MW00891020

The Art of Finishing

in Soccer

Chest Dugger

1

Table Of Contents

About the Author

Chest Dugger is a soccer fan, former professional and coach now looking to share his knowledge. Enjoy this book and several others that he has written.

Free Gift Included

As part of our dedication to help you succeed in your career, we have sent you a free soccer drills worksheet, known as the "Soccer Training Work Sheet" drill sheet. The worksheet is a list of drills that you can use to improve your game and a methodology to track your performance on these drills on a day-to-day basis. We want to get you to the next level.

Click on the link below to get your free drills worksheet.

https://soccertrainingabiprod.gr8.com/

Disclaimer

Copyright © 2022

All Rights Reserved

No part of this eBook can be transmitted or reproduced in any form including print, electronic, photocopying, scanning, mechanical, or recording without prior written permission from the author.

While the author has taken the utmost effort to ensure the accuracy of the written content, all readers are advised to follow information mentioned herein at their own risk. The author cannot be held responsible for any personal or commercial damage caused by information. All readers are encouraged to seek professional advice when needed.

Introduction – The Art of Soccer Finishing

'I was born to score goals, I feel.' Michael Owen.

'You never get fed up scoring goals,' said the English Premier League's all-time leading goal scorer. It's a good job; Alan Shearer did it 260 times. That other fine English exponent of the art, Gary Lineker, feels the same. 'I was only interested in scoring goals,' he said. I wasn't interested in anything else.' It is a passion for the little Argentinian master, Lionel Messi. He is still putting the ball away at the highest level at the age of 34. Of course, the South American's greatest rivals are Brazil. The does not impact on his desire to score. 'It's scoring goals that's great, whether against Brazil or anybody else.'

For Italian bad boy Mario Balotelli, his feats as a goal scorer balanced some of his less salubrious actions. 'You speak bad of me, I score goals,' said the sometime pantomime villain.

Set yourself a small test. Without research, time yourself to name twenty great goalkeepers, twenty great defenders, twenty great midfielders and the same for wingers. Then do the same for strikers. It's a safe bet that the final category will come easiest to the mind.

Spoiler alert – the following paragraph contain some answers to the above question.

The great Brazilian Romario, who netted over 1000 goals during his illustrious career, was clear about the quality a player needed to become a brilliant goal scorer. 'The good attackers only score goals if they have good sex the day before,' he once said. We tend to think that it is a bit more complicated than that. Let's consider the best goal scorers playing today. Robert Lewandowski, still burying chances at 33 while playing at the highest level with German champions Bayern Munich. Of course, those other two evergreens, Cristiano Ronaldo and Lionel Messi must also be regarded as such. Eric Haaland is a much sought-after prize. Perhaps Harry Kane, the Spurs striker and England captain can be included in this list too. Among the now retired category we should include Wayne Rooney and Alan Shearer from England. The diminutive Argentinian, Serge Aguero, also scored many goals, although was less prolific at international level. Thierry Henry is up there with some of the best of all time. Further back we can think of Gerd Muller, the incomparable Pele and the Real Madrid pairing of the (former) mighty Magyar Ferenc Puskas and his companion on the pitch, if not socially, Alberto Di Stefano.

Of course, there are others. But what do these players tend to have in common? Great athleticism and balance of course. Most could score with either foot, are or were good in the air, on top of being skilful dribblers as well. Technically, they were blessed with outstanding natural talent but not only this. They worked at their game constantly, always seeking to improve.

These players had a bit of pace, without exception. And while some, like Thierry Henry, could well have developed a career as a sprinter, others (Puskas particularly comes to mind) might not be able to sustain full speed over half a pitch but were blessed with astonishing acceleration over a short distance. This gave them the ability to create space. They could make room for a shot, or to receive a pass.

Each was a team player. Each one was able to offer a well-placed pass or was willing to make a run to give a team mate a bit of extra time. These days, the best players must also be prepared to work hard. Watch the Egyptian striker Mo Salah, whom many consider to be the best player in the world at the moment. He works constantly to close down opponents, or to make room for a team mate to exploit an opportunity.

The great finishers possess another characteristic. One which is tougher to quantify. Any of us who have played the game at any level will be familiar with that fraction of a second when the ball comes to us, we are ten yards out and the chance to score is there. Our hearts race, our eyes light up… and our technique wobbles under the onslaught of the twin rush that is anticipation and adrenalin. The best finishers are different. They expect to score. It is a surprise to all when they do not. They are ice cool when taking the decisive penalty in a shootout; they are implacable in dealing with a bouncing ball in front of goal; they are deadly when the chance falls to them. Even though they do not put away every opportunity that comes their way, we all expect that they will. Especially themselves.

We can call it extreme self-belief, even arrogance. We can call this determination to score at all costs selfish. But it wins games. All the best finishers possess an element of that belief which tells them they are the best. That nobody else is better. After all, nobody gets excited when they walk through the door of the office, it's their job and as such, an everyday experience. Scoring goals is an everyday experience for a striker. Their business. They can wait for the thrill of closing down the deal, seeing the net bulge and the expression of futility on the face of the keeper. Because, they know it is going to happen.

Yes, the very best finishers are born, and then polished and honed. We cannot all achieve that level. But we can improve our skills, our technique, our mindset. A coach can devise drills and exercises to make their players better in front of goal. After all, if you don't score, you don't win. And that is a goal for everybody who plays soccer.

Many of the following drills, tactics and techniques include diagrams. They have been used to help with clarity in understanding the operation of the exercises. In these, the following symbols are used:

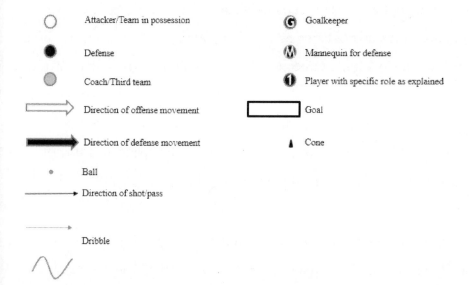

○	Attacker/Team in possession	Ⓖ	Goalkeeper
●	Defense	Ⓜ	Mannequin for defense
◉	Coach/Third team	❶	Player with specific role as explained
⇨	Direction of offense movement	▭	Goal
➡	Direction of defense movement	▲	Cone
∘	Ball		
→	Direction of shot/pass		
⤑	Dribble		

There are specific explanations of symbols by some drills, and they are not drawn to scale.

We'll start with maybe the most important area. The mind of the player. Because if you do not believe you are going to score, cannot control the adrenaline that floods your body the moment the opportunity arises, then you will not be a prolific finisher.

And it is worth reminding readers that whilst a team might only have one or two players who perform up front, all players will from time to time find themselves in a goal scoring position. More so in the fluid game of today, perhaps, than in the past. For some, those opportunities do not come along often; maybe only once every three or four games – for goalkeepers less. Still though, when that rare chance does arise, we need to be able to take it. This book is not just for number nines, it is as much for centre halves, full backs and midfielders. It is for coaches, and lovers of the beautiful game of soccer. A goal is a goal, whoever scores it.

We are beginning to learn that the most important part of the body in scoring those goals is not the foot, or the head. Instead, it is what we find inside the head. The mind.

Changing the Mindset to Finishing

'You have to shoot, to want to score goals no matter how. Just score that goal. You can't be afraid to miss.' Dennis Bergkamp.

A great finisher must know how to miss. How to fail to score. Because that is what they will do for much of the time. So, if a Ronaldo, a Messi, a Haaland, a Lewandowski is going to fail to score more often than they will hit the net, what does that say for players many steps down the ladder? If Harry Kane can shoot wide when it would be easier to hit the target, then our Under Eleven number nine is going to fail even more often. Or the striker from our pub league, giving it his or her all while the remnants of last night's final pint are still sloshing around their insides.

But if Kylian Mbappe, his body blessed with the sort of skills about which the rest of us can only gasp and admire, can become an even better player by developing his mental strength, then so can every player; whatever the level at which they operate.

For those of us who are coaches, we hold an enormous responsibility for ensuring the well-being of our players. Winning is not all; enjoyment is more important than a victory. Comradery is more important than securing three points from the toughest game. Fun outweighs defeating the opposition. Although, winning adds a bit more to all of those; and to win, we must finish off our chances.

Strategy: Getting it Wrong

British cycling dominated the velodrome for close to two decades. It's beginning to come out now, however. With the players getting older, and retiring, the culture of bullying which existed as coaches sought to get an extra ounce out of their elite performers is coming to light.

So let us get this unpleasant elephant in the room out of the way quickly. A coach who bullies their players has no place in the 'beautiful game'. It is no excuse to say that shouting at a young striker, or blaming a defender, makes the team successful. It does not. Long term, damaging the self-esteem of any person will only hamper their progress. When it happens to young players, we impact even more on their mental health.

Strategy: Raising self-esteem

None of the above is meant to imply, in any way, that there is something wrong with seeking improvement. It is how we, as coaches, go about this that matters. Or, if we are players, how we react to setbacks. The following tips are particularly important when coaching youngsters, but the principles still apply if we are in charge of the veteran's team, or the walking football brigade.

Make it fun: When soccer is enjoyable players give more, experiment more, take more risks and learn more about success and failure. Fun is doing, boredom is listening.

Give players control: A crucial one, here. In any walk of life, when we have control of our duties and responsibilities, we perform them better. In terms of soccer, players need a framework in which to perform, but not one that is so rigid that all decision making is taken away from them.

Eliminate failure: We can do this. If we are careful about our definition of failure. Sometimes players will make mistakes. Pertaining to this book, all will miss chances that they should score.

But is that 'failure'? Or is it a step along the pathway to improvement. It is rare to find a player who will not feel an edge of disappointment when they miss a chance that they could – should - score. But by dealing with this positively, helping players to understand how to succeed (be it technique, calming down or even just accepting bad luck or recognising great play by an opponent) we help them to put their miss behind them. To see it as something from which to learn and move on, rather something upon which to dwell.

Neither players nor coaches can eliminate missed chances but promoting a miss as a good thing because it is a lesson learned turns the disappointment on its head. Rewarding the positives of the situation - being in the position to score, being brave enough to take on the shot – mitigates any sense of failure.

Encourage mindfulness: Give time for reflection, encourage visualisation of success.

Encourage support from teammates: No player who has just missed an opportunity wants criticism – they will be giving themselves enough of that. As coach, we can set an example by praising the good and moving on from the bad. A team that has a culture of support rather than criticism will succeed. Players will grow in confidence. Their self-esteem improves. They deal with things that go wrong. They become mentally strong,

Strategy: Developing a culture

Working with players, or even being a player, is often the easy part. There are elements to the wider concept of 'club' or 'team' which are much harder to influence. Any of us who have coached youth teams will know of the nightmare of the pushy parent,

We know the one. Always wants a word at the end; always has a suggestion…one which somehow will see their Jimmy or Jane taking a more major role in proceedings. Albeit, to the detriment of others.

'I really think it would be good for the team if Jimmy were to take free kicks…and penalties…and corners. He's got such a sweet left foot…'

'Don't you think you should abandon this strategy of rotating the captain? It's not working, I've talked to the players, and they'd like Jimmy to be captain every week.'

Meanwhile, little Jimmy or Jane convulses with embarrassment.

'Pass it to Jimmy…pass it to Jimmy. Damn! Why didn't you pass it to Jimmy…he was away and clear…'

Or, worst of all, 'Jane, you are better than that!'

Such parents are vampires to team spirit and therefore mental growth in players. They are very difficult to deal with. They never believe that they are a problem, or that guidelines apply to them. However, we can suggest a strategy to help deal with them.

One: Issue guidelines to all new parents about what is expected at matches. These make it clear that criticism of any player, coach, official or opponent is completely unacceptable.

Two: *Update and resend the guidelines to all parents at least once a season.*

Three: *Where a parent transcends, speak quietly and calmly to them, explaining that although they mean well, and it is great that they are such active supporters, their enthusiasm can be daunting to other players, and even to their own child.*

It takes a particularly bloody-minded parent to continue to transgress after this point, but such people do exist.

Four: *Speak with a partner or peer and ask them to have a word.*

Five: *Issue a formal warning, in writing, stating that unless they are prepared to behave acceptably, they will not be allowed to attend matches or training.*

Six: *Ban them from the club. Sadly, this in turn might involve losing the player as well. Most parents, however, put their children's well-being above their own selfishness. Most. Not all.*

If point six is reached, the matter should be passed to whoever holds responsibility at the club for safeguarding young players.

<u>Here are the key points from the chapter</u>:

We have not spoken very much about finishing per se in this chapter. We are making the point that if we can develop a player's confidence, their self-belief and self-esteem we will make them better finishers because they will not be afraid to miss. Further, we must try to mitigate against negative external influences as well as those the player imposes on themselves.

These points are true of all ages and all levels of player, but they hold particular importance when working with younger players.

Improve players' mental strength and we are well on the way to generating a team who will win. Win, that is, not just in terms of beating their opposition. But also, in terms of their own enjoyment of playing, and the development of their self-esteem. This, in turn, will bring benefits in all aspects of a person's life. There cannot be a bigger victory than that. We can sum this up as below:

- Soccer is about fun more than anything else
- Everything should be geared towards enjoyment
- Players (and coaches) who are happy will progress more, and gain the additional benefits that sport can offer

Now it is time to turn to the skills and techniques which will deliver goals during the game.

Shooting Drills

'I love the game. I love scoring goals.' George Weah.

If we do not shoot, we cannot score. No more needs to be said.

Drill: Basic Shooting Practice

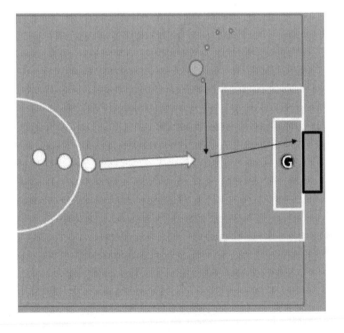

It is essential that players develop good technique when shooting. It is rare in games that there is time and space to prepare for and deliver a shot. Usually, a player will be under pressure, and defenders will be flying in to make a block. Therefore, the best technique must be sufficiently established that it becomes automatic. This drill will help to establish such muscle memory.

Use With: All ages.

Objectives: Perfect technique for shooting

Equipment: Balls and a goal.

Operation of Drill: Coach feeds in a lateral pass towards the D on the penalty area. Attacker runs onto the ball and shoots. Striker retrieves ball if they miss, and then re-joins the line of players.

Key Skills:

- Communication with feeder

- Take one or two touches, shifting the ball slightly to the side of the shooting foot and approximately half a metre to a metre in front
- Run onto the ball
- Plant the non-kicking foot to the side, approximately six to eight inches (fifteen to twenty centimetres) from the ball
- Flex the knee of the non-kicking foot
- Arms out for balance
- Keep the head still, and slightly forwards to shift body weight over the ball
- Glance down at the ball
- Swing the kicking foot smoothly, striking the ball with the laces
- The leg should swing in an arc towards the corner, or point for which the player is aiming (usually the far corner), with ankle locked firm and toes pointing down on contact with the ball
- Follow through smoothly with kicking foot

Development:

- Send feeds from different angles, and at different paces
- Encourage players to try side foot finishes as well as driven finishes (see later chapter for technique.

Drill: Add Some Defence

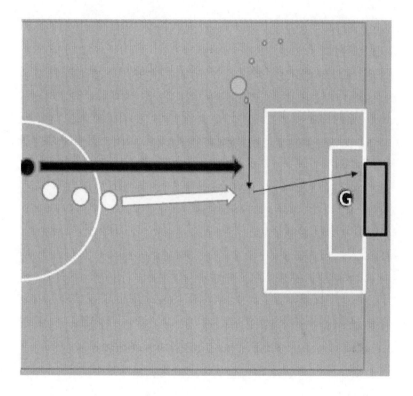

This drill builds on the previous one, but the addition of a defensive player adds pressure on the shooter. Begin with the defender starting behind the striker, ensuring that the striker reaches the ball first. Then close the defenders in, adding pressure to the first touch.

Finally, start the defence from the goal line, allowing them to pressure. This will require the striker to either hit first time or use a skill such as a feint (drop the shoulder, dummy one way while moving the ball with the outside of the opposite foot to create space) before shooting.

However, it is important that players have developed a solid technique before pressure is added so that shooting becomes as much muscle memory as a conscious decision.

Drill: Pass, Move, Shoot.

This drill encourages players to find space through varying the angle of attack. It is particularly useful for developing first time shooting skills, as the player is running on to the ball fast.

Use With: All ages. Ensure players have developed good shooting technique before employing, as an unsure technique will falter with the pace that is imparted in the attack.

Objectives: Running onto the ball.

Equipment: Balls, goal, cones laid out as per diagram.

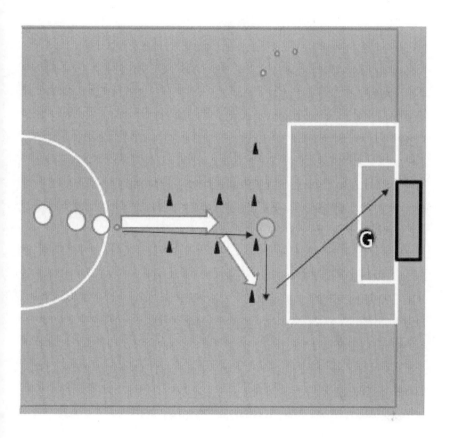

Operation of Drill: Attackers line up from the semi-circle on the halfway line. Each attacker has a ball. Attacker passes firmly to feeder standing on D of penalty area, then follows the ball. The attacker indicates which side they want the lay off, then accelerates in the direction they have indicated, sprinting diagonally. Feeder lays off ball. Striker runs onto ball and hits first time or takes a touch and then shoots.

Key Skills:

- As for shooting above
- Communication from striker, indicating the direction they want the ball laid off
- Drop bodyweight and drive off opposite leg when changing direction, to create space through speed.
- Shoot first time, aiming more centrally as the ball will swing with contact OR
- Take a touch to take oneself forwards and wider, and shoot low and hard across goal to far corner

Development:

- Vary direction and speed of lay off
- Add defence as per the drill above

Drill: Super Shoot

This popular drill is loved by players of all ages. It encourages good technique by allowing a shot to occur while under limited or no pressure. However, there is also an opportunity for shooting under pressure. It is fast paced, and all players should have plenty of action and a chance to score.

Use With: Under eights and upwards. Players must be able to shoot from a reasonable distance for the drill to work.

Objectives: Reinforce shooting technique through plenty of shots, whilst establishing a realistic match situation.

Equipment: Balls - plenty. Two goals. Cones to mark out a halfway line might be useful, especially for younger players whose spacial awareness is less developed.

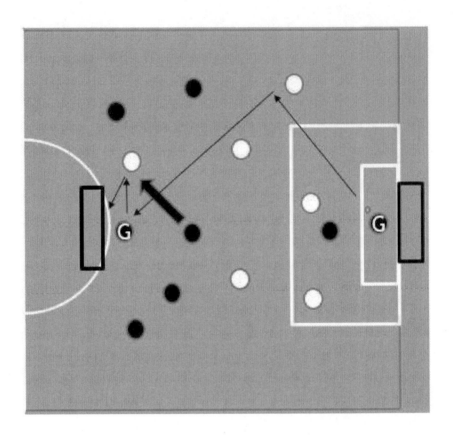

Operation of Drill: Two teams of six including goalkeepers. Set up a playing area either across the width of the pitch or roughly between the edge of the semi-circle and the goal line. Younger players can operate between the edge of the penalty area and the semi-circle. Each team has a goalkeeper, four outfield players in their own half and one outfield player in their opponent's half. This player should be swapped with one of the deeper players at regular intervals.

The play starts with a goalkeeper. They must pass the ball to team mates who set up an opportunity to shoot. Only the opposing attacker in their half is permitted to tackle, although other defenders should shadow the ball from their own half. They will attempt to block shots. Encourage shooting early, looking for power. The attacker in the opponent's half is there for rebounds. They should mostly look to side foot the ball if they get the opportunity, looking for accuracy over power.

After each shot/rebound the opposing keeper begins an attack for their team. This works well if each game has 10 balls, five at each end, and the coach can review after all ten balls have been used.

Key Skills:

- Correct technique for circumstances
- Create space with one or two passes
- Shoot early
- Advance attacker always moving to allow them to get to a rebound first

Development:

- Add a second advanced attacker

Drill: Shooting Chaos

This fun drill does require a bit of setting up and a lot of equipment but is good for encouraging players to have lots of shots from different angles and distances.

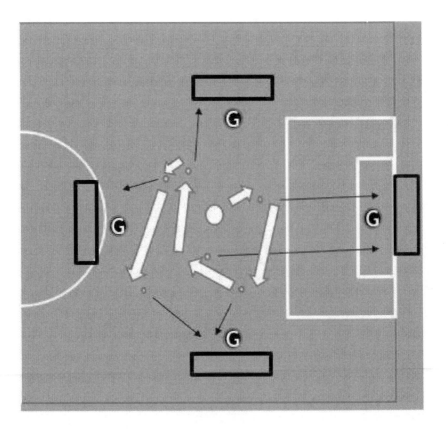

Use With: All ages.

Objectives: Develop accuracy from different angles.

Equipment: Six Balls. Four small goals. Use cones to allow multiple games to happen simultaneously.

Operation of Drill: Create an imaginary square (one could be marked out with cones, but this is not necessary, as the accuracy of the square is not crucial to the drill). Place a goal midway along each line of the perimeter of the square. Each goal has a keeper. Adult players could use half a pitch, approximately. For under 8s the penalty area should be a good size, squared off. Different ages can work with different sizes of squares. Place the six balls randomly inside the square. Players attempt to score as many goals as possible from the six balls in the shortest amount of time. To encourage movement and angle changes, do not allow a player to shoot consecutively at the same goal. After each passage of the drill, swap the shooter with a keeper.

Key Skills:

- Tactical thinking to find the quickest route for shooting
- Movement
- Using good technique at speed
- Varying shot type to circumstance. E.g., a side foot for accuracy from close range shooting, power for more distant shooting, curling for wide shots

Development:

- Add competitive element between players, e.g., number of goals in twenty seconds.
- Make pitch area larger.
- Add a defender to pressure shots.

Here are the key points from the chapter:

- Mostly, a player will be under pressure when shooting
- Given this, technique is paramount
- Technique must be practised until it becomes second nature

In the next chapter we look an area of finished that is becoming increasingly controversial. Heading the ball.

Heading Drills

'As a kid I always wanted to be centre-forward. I wanted the buzz and thrill of scoring goals from an early age.'- Alan Shearer.

It was the early onset of dementia that hit the former England and West Bromwich Albion striker, Jeff Astle, that started it. The elephant in the room. Soccer might be the greatest sport in the world. Heading is without doubt a crucial part of it. But…former players were falling victim to dementia too often. Too early. They were dying too young.

The cause appeared to be the concussive impact of heading the ball. Something had to be done. It is, slowly. We are coaches, or players. Not doctors or scientists. All that we can do is stay up to date with medical findings and follow the guidance we are given. While heading remains such an important part of the game, it is important that players do it properly.

We should, however, limit heading drills during training, or remove them altogether if that is the advice we are given.

Drill: Heading Technique (offensive)

Whilst a defensive header will seek to achieve height and distance, an attacking header is a different beast. Here, the striker will aim to achieve power and accuracy, or even a glance towards the corner. This drill helps younger players overcome common errors and get body position and technique right from the start.

Use With: As young as permitted by your local rules. But even expert players can use the drill as part of a warmup to reinforce key techniques.

Objectives: Perfect technique for downwards headers.

Equipment: Balls. Use soft balls for beginners or those younger players wary of heading the ball.

Operation of Drill: As simple as can be, and deliberately so. This is a short drill which should last no more than two minutes. The focus is totally on heading correctly, and therefore distractions and complexities are completely removed, allowing players to focus on the acquisition and practice of their technique. Simply, players stand approximately five metres apart. One player feeds the ball to the other, using a lob or throw. Their partner headers the ball back, aiming for the toes of their partner.

Key Skills:

- Arms for balance.
- Advance towards the ball, jumping if necessary
- Judge the trajectory of the ball, so that it can be taken at the maximum possible height which allows for a downward header
- Open chest
- Impact the ball on forehead
- Check communication between feeder and player
- Tense neck muscles and thrust head forwards
- Make contact with ball after the forehead has travelled just past the horizontal
- Keep the eyes fixed on the ball
- Other than the head, keep the body still, even if in air

- Aim for the feet of the partner
- Make sure player keeps their eyes open for as long as possible

Development:

- Send feeds from different angles, and at different heights, so player must move
- Try some power headers, with the player pointing their shoulder towards the ball

Drill: Heading for Accuracy

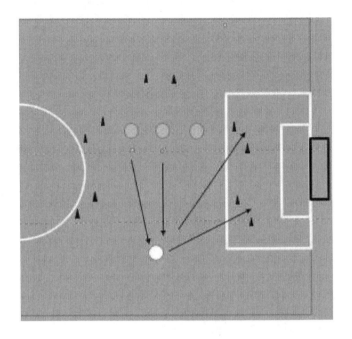

This is a handy drill because it develops technique without putting too much strain on the head, reducing the risk of concussive outcomes.

Use With: Depending on the rules of your football association and league, this is a suitable activity for Under 10s and over. However, keep the number of headers to six maximum per session.

Objectives: Develop technique so that it becomes automatic when employed during the pressure of a match

Equipment: Cones laid out as per diagram, balls.

Operation of Drill: Three feeders lob balls to the playing practising. This player moves to direct the ball between pairs of cones. After two feeds each, players move round a position and the next player moves on to the heading. Feeding happens in a random order.

Key Skills:

- Arms for balance.
- Arch back and project forward on contact with the ball.
- Tense neck muscles for power.
- Point shoulder towards direction of heading for maximum accuracy.
- Work on timing of the header, so the body is still, muscles locked, and body position correct at the point of impact.
- Communication between feeder and player.

- Jump for ball for early connection, ensuring that in a match the defender does not get there first.
- Attack the ball, running onto the feed.

Development:

- Lengthen distance between feeder and player
- Change position of target cones to develop flick ons and glancing headers

Drill: Hitting the Corners

Headers which hit the corners are far more likely to result in a goal. We also practise the glancing header with this drill, which can often lead to a goal at the far post, even if the header itself is not on target.

Use With: The drill is quite challenging, so it is best employed with adults, older youth teams and particularly talented younger players.

Objectives: Create goal scoring opportunities by heading into the corners.

44

Equipment: Two cones, balls.

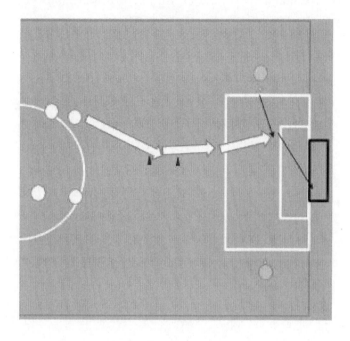

Operation of Drill: Two cones are positioned close to the penalty area. Players line up to either side of the rear most cone. Players alternately from these lines. They make a diagonal run to the first cone, straighten up then break into another diagonal run after the second cone. They head towards the near post. Feeder lobs ball in, and shouts 'Near' or 'Far'. These are the posts towards which the player must direct their header.

Key Skills:

- Accelerate onto the ball.
- Concentrate on attacking the ball, maintaining correct body position.
- For the near post header, that is, the header aimed back towards the near post:
  - Arms for balance
  - Project the head forward on contact
  - Aim to get above the ball to head downwards
- For the header glanced towards the far post:
  - Attack the ball
  - Rotate head towards far post on contact with the ball.
  - Whilst still using the forehead for contact, aim to glance the ball instead of achieving full contact

Development:

- Have players from both lines attack together
- Communication between players
- One attacks near post, one far post
- Far post player stays onside ready for the glancing header if it is not on target

- Introduce a goalkeeper
- Introduce defenders, but do not allow them to compete for the ball with juniors, for safety reasons.

Drill: Creating Space

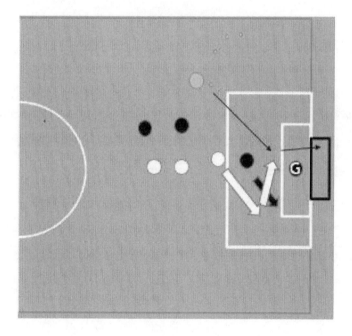

Heading the ball when in space is both easier and more likely to result in a goal. This simple drill helps train players to make runs automatically and find space.

Use With: Finding space is a crucial skill in soccer, so use this drill with players as young as possible within your FA's regulations.

Objectives: Make space finding runs an automatic weapon in a player's arsenal.

Equipment: Balls. With younger or less experienced players cones can be used to help players adopt the correct starting positions.

Operation of Drill: The coach stands wide. The attacker makes a run to the far post, then darts back to the near post. The defender goes with the attacker. The attacker then cuts back towards the near post, accelerating as the ball comes in. For safety, the goalkeeper and defender must allow the striker a free header. The striker attacks the ball and attempts to score. The attacker then moves to the defensive line, the defender to the offensive line, ready for their next turn. After everybody has had a go, switch runs so the dummy is to the near post, before breaking to the far post. Finally, allow the striker to choose their run, and encourage communication with the feeder.

Key Skills:

- The dummy run is at half or two-thirds pace so the change of pace on the attacking run creates space.
- Drop centre of balance, and pump legs hard to create space on the attacking run.
- Some legal contact with the defender can help to create a bit more space.
- Attack the ball.
- Decide early whether to glance the ball to the far post, or power it to the near post.
- Communication between feeder and player.
- Jump the ball for early connection.
- Attack the ball, running onto the feed.

Development:

- With younger or less experienced players, begin without a defender.

Drill: 3 v 3 Game

Everybody loves a game when they are developing skills. This is a good one, with small enough numbers to ensure that every player gets sufficient chance to work on their heading. For youth levels, players should be allowed a free header, that is, defenders may not head the ball at all. At adult level, allow the defensive team to head the ball, but not to challenge an offensive header. The risk of head injury is too great to allow competition for the ball at this point.

Use With: Depending on the rules of your football association and league, this is a suitable activity for Under 11s and over. However, the skill level of the players must be high enough that they can chip or flick a cross for a player to run onto and head. If they can only lift the ball by driving it, then they are not ready for the drill.

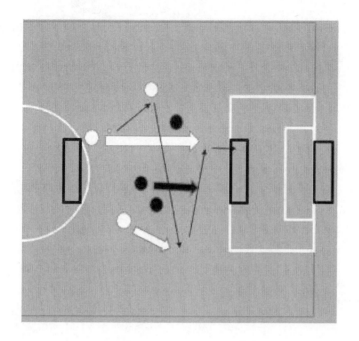

Objectives: Develop technique in a semi competitive setting.

Equipment: Two goals, one set on the D of the penalty area, the other on the semi-circle of the halfway line. One ball.

Operation of Drill: Three versus three. One team start with the ball, they must pass it wide. The wide player crosses, for a team mate to head into the empty goal. The other team then begins with the ball. Play first team to score ten goals, or for a five-minute match. No tackling. Limit players to one metre from an opponent. No tackling and no heavy pressure.

Key Skills:

- Make well timed runs into the goal scoring area.
- Communication with crosser.
- Focus on heading technique.

Development:

- Allow greater pressure during the build-up.

Here are the key points from the chapter:

- Safety is all when it comes to heading
- Data and research are improving all of the time
- We ignore this at our peril. More significantly, at our players' peril

A Short message from the Author:

Hey, are you enjoying the book? I'd love to hear your thoughts!

Many readers do not know how hard reviews are to come by, and how much they help an author.

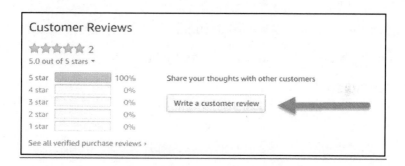

I would be incredibly thankful if you could take just 60 seconds to write a brief review on Amazon, even if it's just a few sentences!

Thank you for taking the time to share your thoughts!

Your review will genuinely make a difference for me and help gain exposure for my work.

Speed off the Mark

'As a kid I always wanted to be centre-forward. I wanted the buzz and thrill of scoring goals from an early age.' Alan Shearer.

The ability to find the burst of pace to create space and time for a shot is a key attribute of a good finisher. Reading the game forms part of this. Knowing where to run and when to do so is hard to teach. It comes with experience, and when players study professionals in their positions.

We would always advocate a coach encouraging their players to watch soccer on TV, and if it is practicable and affordable, to attend professional matches. From this comes an understanding of how to gain that fraction of a second's advantage that might allow a clean shot, rather than one under pressure.

This is not always possible, however, and in this chapter we look at some of the drills and other factors that might give our players an edge in this department.

Of course, if a player is blessed with the speed of a Ronaldo, a Mbappe or a Thierry Henry, then that is a rare blessing. Unfortunately, though, even the best coach cannot instil pure pace where it does not naturally occur. But what the best coaches do is to fine tune a player's speed, developing it where it is most effective.

We are concentrating on speed in finishing in this chapter, but the drills are equally as useful for defensive players. Again, the ability of a centre half to nip in front of their striker, or a central defensive midfielder to get close enough to their runner to make a challenge, can each contribute towards a match winning performance.

Technique: Maximising Speed Off the Mark

- Get the leg positions right. It forms a backwards Z shape, with the upper leg forming the top line of the Z, the lower leg the more horizontal line and the foot the bottom line. The calf muscle reaches up to the hamstring
- The leg drives directly down, with short strides making contact with the ground in line with the hips

- Stay in contact with the ground for a short time, and drive off
- A low centre of gravity will generate the very initial speed, but in an extended sprint, the body should be horizontal, and the head still
- The stride will lengthen naturally as speed is generated, but it is important that the stride continues to strike the ground in line with the hips. By overextending, power is lost, and a stride in front of the body acts as a break to momentum
- Arms should pump forward and back, not side to side

Drill: Forwards and Backwards

This drill mimics the actions of a striker who is moving slowly backwards to offer an easier pass to a teammate. The striker then explodes in a different direction, quickly easing into full sprint mode.

Use With: All ages. Children can improve their speed by learning to sprint correctly.

Objectives: Create space with a change of pace and direction.

Equipment: Cones in pairs, approximately   apart.

Operation of Drill: Very simple. Players jog backwards between cones, then accelerate forwards in the opposite direction.

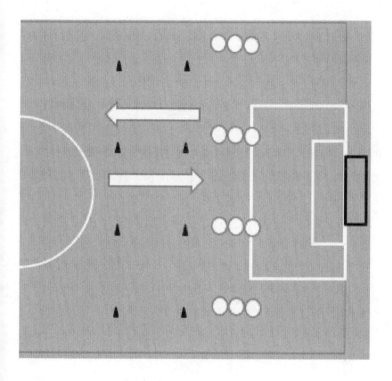

Key Skills:

- Getting the technique correct for the change of pace

Development:

- Add a third cone which offers a different direction for the change of pace
- With younger players, run the drill as a relay to maintain excitement

Drill: Speed Varieties (with ball)

Speed training should be a part of every session. Once loosened up, experienced players can use the following drills to complete their warm ups. When undertaking speed training, allow a little jogging between activities.

Look to repeat each activity three to five times per player and use three to five so different activities in a training stint. Once players become familiar with speed training exercises, they can run through them quickly.

The following drills include four different activities, with groups moving quickly through their ten repetitions, and then moving onto the next speed drill in line.

A ball is used because, after all, these are soccer training sessions!

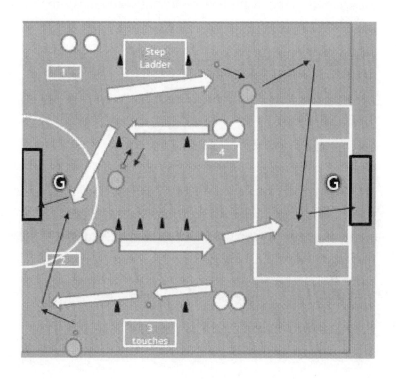

Use With: All ages. Younger players will respond best to simple activities. The rule is 'Do; not Listen or Watch.' Keeping our younger teams active is the key to good coaching.

Objectives: Developing speed while working with a ball.

Equipment: Bag of balls. Cones, pairs about 10 metres apart. (Where more cones are used in a drill, the end two should be 10 metres apart, the remainder spread evenly between these two). Two goals.

Operation of Drill: Set up the four sets of cones. Work across the pitch, or between the half way line and the goal line, as per the diagram. Divide the players into four groups. One for each activity, through which they rotate after each three to five repetitions each. Two keepers are needed, three coaches or feeders. Somebody will need to ensure there is a supply of balls where they are needed. Each pair of cones supports a speed drill activity.

Speed Activity One and Two

These two work in conjunction. In Activity One, use a sprint (sometimes called a 'pace') ladder. This is very useful for developing drive at the outset of a sprint. Players must pump their legs with short, hard strides.

The player sprints through the ladder, then plays a layoff, or wall pass, with a coach. The player then accelerates into space for the return. The player from Activity One crosses across the penalty area to a player from Activity Two.

This player has run alongside the four to seven (depending on age of player) cones in their drill. These drills are to develop an even stride pattern. Players land their feet in line with each cone.

Once through the cones, they run on to finish the cross provided by the player from Activity One

Speed Activity Three and Four

These activities work in the opposite direction to One and Two, leading to attacks on the other goal. Activity Three helps to work on leg control. Players run to a ball placed midway between their two cones. They move to lightly touch the top of the ball with the sole or their feet, alternating left foot, right foot. They make six touches of the ball then sprint on. A coach feeds a pass and the player runs on and crosses.

Meanwhile, the player from activity four is seeking to arrive to finish the cross off with a shot on goal. The player has sprinted forwards, stopped just prior to the final cone to exchange a pass with a coach. He or she returns the pass then sprints on for the cross, judging their arrival for just the right time to meet the cross.

Repeat the drills until each player has complete the set amount (up to ten, depending on time). Then rotate to the next speed skill.

Key Skills:

- Communication. The drills must be completed at speed, but in a way that allows the players to work together
- Apply sprinting technique outlined above
- Work at speed, but with enough control to remain effective on the ball. This may involve slowing a little on approach to the ball

Development:

- Use different drills.

Resources: Training Equipment

There are a number of resources which a club can purchase to help speed work. They are good but do have their drawbacks. Firstly, they are expensive. Secondly, they do not lend themselves to group activities (hence the variety of activities in the drill above).

Sprint ladders are among the best resources in which a club can invest. Parachutes, which provide resistance in sprint work, developing muscle groups, are also good. Rubber bungee harnesses offer similar effects.

We would not recommend investing in the latter two here if we are working with a team of young players. Parachutes and harnesses can be time consuming to put on, and if players need assistance donning them, a sprint session turns into no more than dressing up time.

Facilities: Using the Environment for Low-Cost Training

However, many training grounds have small inclines around the outside of them. If we are lucky enough to have such an incidental facility, it is perfect for sprint work. Running up an incline offers a great workout for the muscles, developing power in the legs. Provided the hill is not too steep, it can also provide useful downhill running. Extra speed is gained, and the runner must concentrate more fully on technique in order to maintain control.

It is important that downhill work is undertaken on the slightest slope. Chaos, and more seriously, injuries will follow if activity is not risk assessed and well supervised.

<u>Here are the key points from the chapter</u>:

- Sprinting to create space is a key skill in the arsenal of the expert finisher
- Speed can be developed, at least to an extent
- This is particularly the case in the five to ten metre burst which is vital to a good finisher
- Technique must be studied and applied
- Drills can enhance this skill further - it is worth practising
- Although equipment can help, we can also use our environment to assist speed development

Next, we will consider the vital nature of players being comfortable using both feet to finish.

Using Both Feet to Shoot

'To be the key player in creating and scoring goals, that's what I take pride in, and the thing I know how to do best.' Tiffeny Milbrett

An aim for any player is to be as comfortably using one foot as the other. The ability to achieve this opens a myriad of opportunities for the player. Suddenly, both wings become serious options for play; it becomes easier to create space, since it is available on both sides of the body; opportunities for passing and shooting both become more viable, since there is no requirement to shift the ball, or body, to open up the stronger foot.

Of course, being two footed becomes even more important when shooting on goal. This is often to the point at which there is least time, and most need to react quickly. Being two footed gives a player far more opportunity to score.

As coaches, we should include some use of the weaker foot in every session. As players, if we want to become the best we can, we should work with our weaker foot until it stops being that. Starting young is the key. Those with responsibilities for under six or under seven sides have an extra responsibility for helping their young charges to become two footed. Because, even by the age of five, young children will naturally favour one side over the other. By the age of twelve, change is very, very difficult to bring about.

Drill: Practising Technique

The issue with using both feet, for most one-footed players, is that using their weaker foot feels uncomfortable. This is because technique is weak. As coaches, we have a duty to improve a player's all-round ability, and that includes encouraging them to be two footed. At the same time, if achieving this was as simple as just working on that weaker foot, then every coach and every player would set this as a goal.

For the most able, the most committed and the most single minded, such an approach will probably work. For many, though it will not. Players – young and old – need to feel success in what they are practising, and they also need to enjoy it.

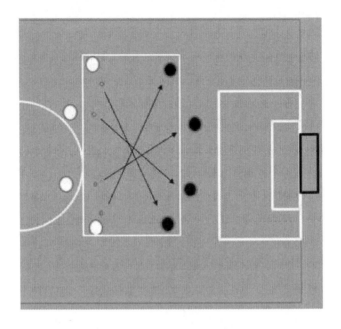

This is where this drill comes into its own. It is active and fun.

Use With: All ages. The organised chaos of the drill makes it popular with children.

Objectives: Work on the weaker foot.

Equipment: Cones to mark out a grid approximately 20 metres x 10 metres. Balls.

Operation of Drill: Eight players position themselves around the outside of the grid, two on each side. Players drive low shots across the grid to the player on the opposite angle. One touch to control, and then the shot is returned. Players aim to time the shot for accuracy, and also to avoid hitting another player's shot crossing the grid. Note: players are not aiming to drive the ball past their partner. Their partner is placed to represent a shot to a corner, and as such a player should aim to shoot directly to this partner. Note: Players only shoot with their weaker foot.

Key Skills:

- Maintain technique for shooting
- Concentrate on shooting for power, using the laces.
- Aim across the grid, to mimic aiming for the corners of the goal.

Development:

- Introduce firm side foot shooting.

Drill: Six Player Drill

Here we move towards a more realistic situation to practise shooting with the weaker foot.

Use With: Under nines upwards. Players need to be old enough to hold themselves in their space.

Objectives: Work on the weaker foot while being placed under pressure.

Equipment: Cones to mark out a grid approximately 30 metres x 10 metres. More cones to divide this grid into three zones of approximately 10 metres x 10 metres. Balls.

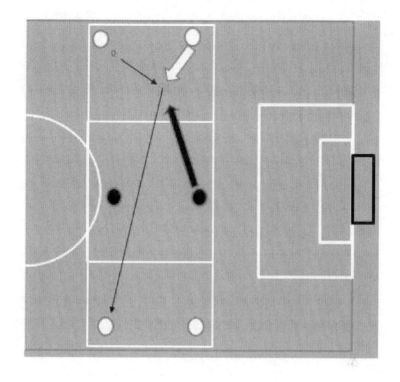

Operation of Drill: Six players divide into three groups of two. (The drill can be adapted to work with three groups of three as well.) Each group is given a small grid in which to work. Play begins with a player in an end grid. A pass is made in front of their partner. Their partner runs onto the ball and shoots first time using their weaker foot. Meanwhile, one of the two players in the central grid, moves forward into the shooting grid to pressure the ball. Note, shooting accuracy is achieved by hitting towards the team at the other end. No physical goal is involved. Once the shot is completed, the drill is repeated from the opposite end.

If a defender intercepts, they lay the ball back to the passer from the grid that has just taken the shot. Swap positions after three or four minutes so all players have a turn as defender. (This drill does work with shooting using the stronger foot as well.)

Key Skills:

- Maintain technique when under pressure.
- Concentrate on shooting for power, using the laces.
- Or accuracy using the side foot. However, the ball must be played as a shot, not a pass.
- Aim to shoot at an angle.
- Getting the body into position to shoot first time.
- Passing sympathetically to allow a player to run onto the ball and shoot first time.
- Pressurising the ball, approaching quickly but under control.

Development:

- Set up targets at either end, to encourage shooting for accuracy and across the grid.

Drill: Dribble and Shoot

Players, especially younger ones, love dribbling. This is an active drill with several players working at once.

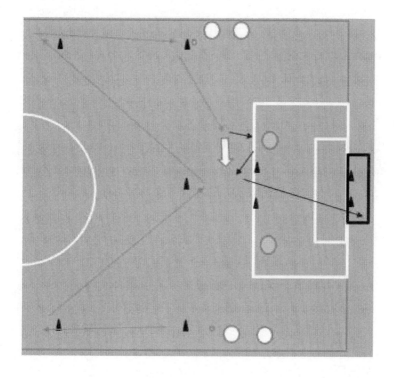

Use With: All ages.

Objectives: Make use of the weaker foot feel natural.

Equipment: Cones to mark out the playing area as per the diagram. Two cones to make a shooting gate. Cones to split the goal into three zones, to encourage shooting for the corner. Balls.

Operation of Drill: There are two groups of players, one by each of the wide cones. Two additional players are used to provide the feed. A player dribbles to the cone away from the goal, cuts back towards the central cone, heads up to the opposite corner and back to the opposite starting point. The player then drives on an angle towards the goal. The player lays of a pass to the feeder and continues their run towards the two cone 'shooting gate'. The feeder lays a pass into their path. The player advances onto the ball and shoots, either first time or after one touch, using whichever foot is best (i.e. left foot if driving in from the right, and right foot if driving in from the left.) They aim to shoot into the corners.

Each time a player reaches a cone, set off another player from the opposite side of the pitch. This ensures many players are active at the same time.

Key Skills:

- Dribbling using two feet to turn, and the laces for running at pace.
- Laying off an accurate pass.
- Adjusting pace to run onto the shot.
- Shooting with both feet.

Development:

- Introduce a goalkeeper. This works best with two keepers taking alternate shots. It is good practice for the keeper as they have little time to recover from their previous shot.
- Get players to add a skill during their dribble. For example, a step over, or feint.

Match Play: Change the Foot

Every coach knows that there is nothing like a game at the end of a session to practice the skills covered during the session. Even seasoned professionals like to finish with a five a side, so it becomes even more important for younger players. Keep sides small to encourage lots of touches on the ball.

This match is a controlled one. The coach shouts out 'Left', 'Right' or 'Alternate', changing every thirty seconds or so. Players must use the foot called. 'Alternate' means just as it says, they must use a different foot for each touch.

Here are the key points from the chapter:

- Two footed players are more effective players
- It is possible to make a player competent with both feet
- Doing so is hard work. But it is easier if we start young

Another exciting skill next. Volleying!

Volleying Skills and Drills

'Everybody tries to score a great goal, and I am lucky I have netted a few.' Zlatan Ibrahimovic.

If a goal is the most exciting, dramatic moment in soccer, then when that goal comes from a volley, the thrill is even greater. There are many kinds of volleys, from the carefully judged, side footed clearance from a central defender to the explosive scissor kick or unlikely overhead shot.

All are volleys. We'll look at the last two of these in a later chapter, but here we will concentrate on the standard volley shot. Still spectacular, still a great challenge to master, but the sort of chance that comes along often enough to make it an essential part of every great finisher's locker.

A volley is a strike of the ball while it is still in the air. To be successful, it requires balance, control and early decision making.

Technique: Mastering the Volley as a shot

- A player must make up their mind as quickly as possible that they are going to attempt a volley. This is because they require as much time as possible to get their body in position
- Picture the point of contact with the ball, judging its arc. Usually, this will be slightly further away from the body than with a shot from the ground. Ideally, a player will strike the ball at the lowest point of its reachable trajectory
- Fix the head on that spot. Having one's head as still as possible will help ensure the best body shape
- Bring the arms up for balance
- Plant the non-kicking foot so that it is slightly behind and to the side of the perceived strike zone.
- Lead the strike with the knee of the kicking foot
- Bring the striking foot through behind the knee and begin to extend the lower leg
- Point the toes slightly downwards
- Lock the ankle

- Control the speed of leg movement; too fast and accuracy of the strike is lost
- Aim for the middle or upper part of the ball
- Strike the ball with the leg slightly bent
- A strike with the instep will be more accurate
- A strike with the laces more powerful
- In either case, follow through smoothly, ensuring that the arms stay out for balance
- Ensure the head is over the ball to stop the shot flying over the bar

Easy! Or not. Therefore, a lot of practice is required to master this technique. A major difference between a volley and a shot is that in the latter, it is necessary to generate pace, especially if the ball is stationary or moving slowly. With a volley, the ball naturally has pace (or it would be on the ground) so control becomes far more important than hitting the ball hard. Even with a drill, the sight of a goal fills a player with adrenalin, and the desire to burst the net takes over. Especially with younger players. Therefore, it is a good idea to work on technique without using a goal in the early stages. Once technique is established, then the fun can really start!

Drill: Establishing Technique

This is an enjoyable yet simple drill. We can enliven it with the addition of a goalkeeper, which younger players will particularly enjoy.

Use With: All ages.

Objectives: Perfecting the volleying technique.

Equipment: Cones to mark out a square or circle, around 10 metres across. Ball.

Operation of Drill: One player along each side of the grid. A keeper in the centre (optional). Players volley from their hands across the grid to a team mate. They must aim to stop the keeper from intercepting but control the volley sufficiently that their team mate can control the ball. Two points if the team can control the ball using an outfield legal part of the body, one point if they have to use their hands. No points if the keeper intercepts, or the ball goes past its target.

The player who receives the volley then picks the ball up to volley it to another player.

Key Skills:

- Follow the technique outlined above
- Volley with sufficient control to allow the team mate to stop the ball

Development:

Add in players and take out the option to use hands. Now players must keep the ball off the ground using headers, chests, knees or volleys. They may play the ball to themselves but must make a pass for it to count as a point.

Drill: Volleying from Throw Ins

We'll set up three drills now to practise situations which are likely to occur in matches. For the first two, the players are volleying from distance and should drive through the ball using the laces. For the third, the players are volleying from much closer in, and should side foot for accuracy since if they hit the target, they are likely to score from such a range.

Use With: All ages.

Objectives: Approach the ball correctly to volley first time.

Equipment: Balls. Mannequin (optional).

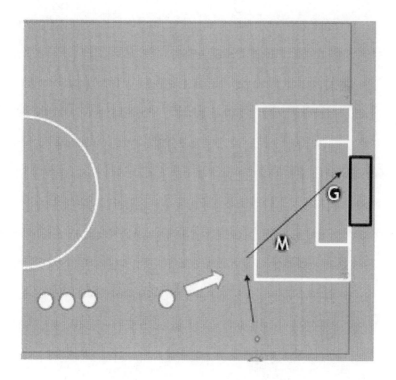

Operation of Drill: The coach or a team mate takes a throw in laterally from the corner of the penalty area. The player practising the volley times their run to strike the bouncing ball and volley it across the goal. A mannequin can be used to make the volley more challenging. A goalkeeper can also be introduced to make the drill more interesting for the players.

Key Skills:

- Timing the run to reach the ball as it drops towards the ground following a bounce
- Striking through the ball with a smooth follow through
- Aiming across the goal to avoid the mannequin

Development:

- With more advanced players, encourage them to take the volley before the bounce. Here the ball is coming from a higher trajectory, so the skill is more difficult.
- Encourage players to strike fully through the ball to introduce dip.

84

- Allow players to experiment hitting across the ball to induce swerve

Drill: Volleying from Clearances/Waiting on the edge of the Box

We will look at corner and free kicks later, but it is always worth positioning a player on the edge of the box from these situations. Their job is not to run in and head the ball but wait for clearances where they can shoot from range. With many bodies in front of them, the keeper is often unsighted in these situations, or deflections can occur off of defenders or strikers, leading to goals.

In these situations, a defender will usually be seeking to charge down the shooter, meaning they must get their shot off quickly. That in turn means competence with volleying is essential in a player who undertakes this edge of the box role.

Use With: All ages.

Objectives: Volley first time, or after chest/knee control, on a ball that is coming directly towards you.

Equipment: Balls. Mannequins to represent a crowded penalty area. These can be substituted with players, although beware of injury with shots flying around.

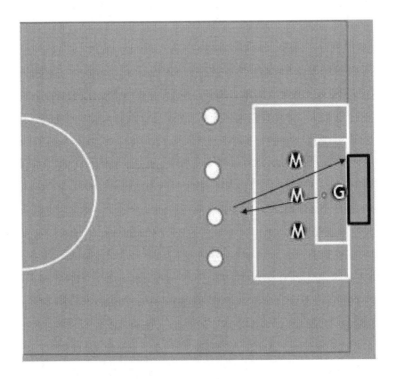

Operation of Drill: Attackers spread just beyond the edge of the box. The more attackers, the greater number of angles can be used for shooting. The keeper starts with the ball and lobs it out towards one of the attackers. The lob imitates a punch out or headed clearance, so it should be high, not too powerful and dropping.

The nearest attacking player calls for the shot, and attacks the ball, judging the best moment for the strike.

Key Skills:

- Communication
- Rapid judgement of whether they are the best placed player to take on the volley
- Attacking the ball
- Hitting the target (This is, of course, always important, but becomes more so in this situation. If the keeper has a clear view of a shot, they will often save it. However, in this situation, their view could well be obscured, plus there is the chance of a deflection. Therefore, a shot on target has a greater chance of scoring. The relationship between accuracy and power shifts towards the former.)

Development:

- Introduce a defender to charge down the ball

Drill: Volley from a cross

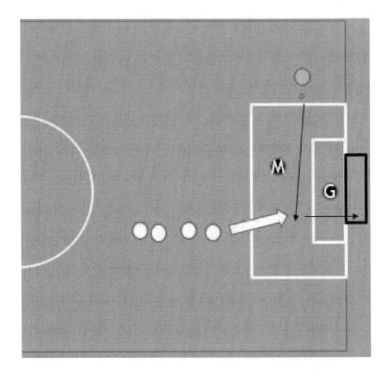

In this drill, the player is volleying from close range. The keeper is unlikely to stop the shot if it is on target. The most accurate method of shooting involves using the instep. Therefore, volleys here occur with the instep.

Use With: All ages.

Objectives: Volley a ball coming across the body. Volley with accuracy.

Equipment: One or two mannequins to represent defenders who can obscure clear sight of the cross. Balls.

Operation of Drill: A feeder lobs the ball across the penalty area, broadly in line with the penalty spot. The keeper is optional, but in order to avoid injury and allow the main focus of the drill to operate, i.e. volleying, should remain in their six yard box. A striker runs onto the ball just inside the far post.

They must strike the volley first time, using their instep. (See technique above).

Key Skills:

- Timing the run
- Volleying with control rather than power
- Head over the ball to ensure it does not fly over the bar

Development:

- Play in crosses with the feet, so the ball has more pace and is therefore harder to volley, but more like the match situation

Tactic: Finishing at the far post

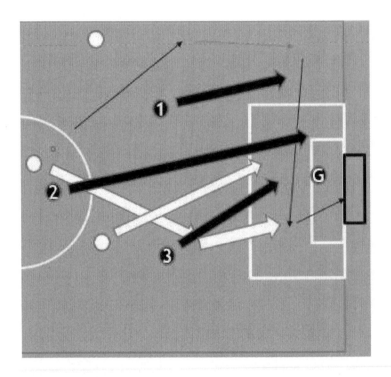

This tactic can be used in a three v three scenario, where a player in possession has time to hit an accurate pass wide. The aim is to draw defenders towards the ball, creating space for a striker arriving to finish with a side foot shot or volley.

Stage One: The player in possession knocks a long pass wide to a winger supporting the break. Defender one (above) must track this player as the nearest defender.

Stage Two: The player making the play draws diagonally away towards the opposite edge of the penalty area, making them the player of least danger.

Stage Three: The final supporting attacker makes a dynamic and deep run towards the near post. Their defender (three) must track this run, as it is the most likely situation from which a goal will result.

Stage Four: The other defender, four, is now left with a dilemma. Do they track the original passer, or do they drive back with a view to cutting out any resultant cross? Effectively, they must opt to head back cut out the cross. If they do not, and defender one is beaten by the winger, then that winger has a clear run on goal, and can pull the ball back for a likely score, as the keeper will be forced to move out to cover their near post.

Stage Five: The winger does not seek to beat their defender, but instead crosses from wide. In doing so, they take out all three defenders, but only the attacker who made their run towards the near post.

Stage Six: The original passer now has time to attack the far post, which will be unguarded. The keeper will also be out of position, as they will have been drawn towards their near post. The most likely cross not to be cut out is a lifted cross, as this will curl around the defence and away from the keeper. The striker is therefore likely to be required to finish with a side foot volley.

Coaching Point: Explain and set up the scenario. This can be developed in a six a side match with limits. Here, each team has two strikers who must remain in their opponents half, and two defenders who must remain in their own (plus a keeper). Only the midfielder is permitted to play in both halves and will therefore be the spare player who arrives to score. Count any goal scored used the tactic above as two points, and any other goal as one point.

Match Practice: Headers and Volleys

Why not? The great favourite of the kickaround in the park is a low pressure way of practising the volley. With younger children, or even adults, it is best to limit the heading element. For those unfamiliar with the perennial practice, there is a goalkeeper, a ball, a goal and some players. And that's about it. One or two players provide flicks, lobs and crosses, and players attempt to score volleys. Technique begins to become automatic. The game is popular with any age, including adults. The only requirement is that the players are old enough and able enough to put in crosses.

Here are the key points from the chapter:

- Finishing with a volley is admittedly rare
- But drilling to improve volleying is fun
- Soccer is about fun
- Drills to improve volleying therefore have a value beyond the skill itself

In the next chapter we will enter into the mazy world of finishing off a dribbling run.

Dribble and Finish Drills

'Scoring goals is like making love: everyone can do it, but nobody does it like me.' Alfredo Di Stefano.

There are many aspects of soccer that get the crowd onto their feet, the heart racing and the adrenaline flowing. A spectacular shot, an incisive pass (surely, something as close to high art as the sporting world can offer?), a great save…

And a superb, mazy, dribbling run. When that dribble ends with a goal, it is even more exciting.

Drill: Creating Space for the Shot when Dribbling (Feint/Stepover)

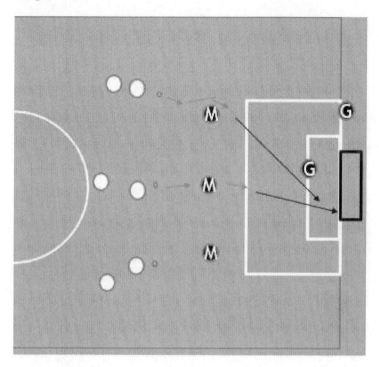

This drill is fast paced, with players attacking a mannequin (or stationary defender), beating them with skill, or opening up space for the shot, then shooting past the keeper.

Use With: All ages.

Objectives: Create enough space to get a shot away.

Equipment: Three mannequins. Balls.

Operation of Drill: Players line up in three groups across the pitch. Mannequins are placed just outside the penalty box. One keeper plays, with a second to rotate in if desired. Players dribble at the mannequin, then use a skill to create space for the shot. Technique for the step over, feint, change of pace and hook turn are listed below this drill.

Key Skills:

- Run at three quarters pace, before accelerating
- Employing the skill to create space
- Shooting quickly once the space is created, aiming across goal for the corners.

Development:

- Replace the mannequin with an active defender
- Introduce a team mate to attack the far post for rebounds or crosses

Techniques to Beat a Defender

It is not essential to have great pace in order to create space for a shot when dribbling. What is more important is guile.

- Approach defender at three quarters pace
- Dribble with the laces, using short, light steps
- Decide early which technique will be used
- Maintain balance as the defender backs away

Step Over

- Use your leading foot to step across and over the ball, dropping your shoulder in the direction of the foot movement
- Plant this foot, then drag the ball sideways with the outside of the other foot
- Use this second foot to knock the ball forwards at about sixty degrees
- Accelerate at full pace into the space created
- Shoot

- Practice using multiple stepovers with alternate feet (watch videos of Ronaldo at his best, from his younger days when he played as a winger!)
- When the defender's weight has shifted completely to the side, complete the final stepover and move away to shoot of continue your dribble

Feint

- Drop your shoulder and step firmly to one side
- 'Give the eyes' – that is, look at the space to this side, as though that is where you are headed
- Use the outside of the other foot to knock the ball forwards at about sixty degrees to the other side of the player
- Accelerate hard into the space created
- Dribble on or shoot

Change of Pace

- Knock the ball past the defender

- Accelerate rapidly onto the ball, using this change of pace to create the space required
- Shoot

Hook Turn

This is especially useful when running wide on the 'wrong' side. That is, down the left for a right footer, and down the right for a left footer. The hook turn creates a little space and brings the balls onto your stronger foot ready for the shot or cross.

- Use a change of pace to knock the ball on the outside of the defender
- Use the outside of 'inner' foot to stop the ball. That is, the right foot if on the left or the left foot if on the right
- Use the same foot and same movement to drag the ball back close to one hundred and eighty degrees
- Use the same foot to knock the ball at around 45 degrees, or less, in the direction of goal. If planning a shot, this 45 degree turn should take you back towards the half way line a little way.
- Knock the ball on for another touch if time

- Accelerate at full speed
- You will now be inside the defender, with your body protecting the ball
- Keeping the arms out for balance and protection, steady yourself
- Sweep the ball firmly with the instep, and the shot or cross will curve towards the far post.

Technique: One on One with the Keeper (Wide and Straight)

There are various options available to strikers when they find themselves through on the keeper. The ability to stay in control, make up one's mind and execute calmly is the difference between players who mostly score in this situation, and those who mostly miss.

With so many options, the player must make up their mind quickly how they plan to finish the move. A **glance** to check around is the first step. The player asks themselves questions to assess the situation. How much pressure is there from the nearest defender? Do I have support from a team mate? Where am I in relation to the goal? Wide or central?

Once these questions are answered, the player decides on their finish. If a team mate is in support, most good finishers will seek to use them, either to draw the keeper and pass into space, or to use them as a dummy to allow them to finish the move themselves.

If a defender is close by, this limits opportunities a little. Here, the striker will seek to position their body between defender and ball. Doing so makes a tackle very difficult, because if the defender commits a foul in that situation, they will most probably receive a red card or give away a penalty. Possibly both.

Options:

Round the Keeper

- Reduce to three quarters pace
- Use a skill, such as a feint, stepover, or drag back to create space to beat the keeper
- Give the eyes, to draw the keeper to one side, while moving the ball to the other

- Remember, the keeper can use their hands, so can cover a much wider area. Therefore, the movement past them needs to be exaggerated

Shoot Early

- If the keeper is not set, shooting early, that is from the edge of the penalty area, can be a successful tactic
- The keeper will probably be moving forwards to narrow the angles to their goal
- Shoot hard and low, using the side foot for accuracy
- If space is available to the corners, then aim there. If not, a driven shot close to the keeper's legs is a good tactic. The keeper will try to make themselves as big as possible, which makes it difficult for them to get their hands to the area close to their body
- An accurate shot through the legs often results in a goal

Chip the Keeper

- If running directly at the keeper from a central position, this is a useful tactic, especially if the keeper is set.

- Where the keeper is set, they will be low, with arms and legs wide to make themselves as big as possible
- Try a dummy. Either semi pause or set to shoot but do not carry it through.
- When the keeper goes to ground, hit the ball low down using the instep, and leaning slightly backwards
- It is not necessary to input too much pace on the chip, as doing so might lift the ball over the bar

Draw the Keeper and Pass into Space

- Where a teammate is in support, drive towards the opposite post.
- Draw the keeper towards the post, opening the goal up
- Pass across the goal, ensuring the teammate is level or behind the ball (to avoid offside)
- If the keeper does not commit to covering their post, simply slot the ball into this space with a low, hard shot using the instep

Draw the Foul

Sometimes, a striker is running fast onto the ball, and the keeper is advancing. In this situation there may not be time to steady oneself for a shot, or sufficient space to take a touch.

Here, seek to get a toe to the ball before the diving keeper. Lift both feet from the ground to prevent injury and accept the contact. The move should result in a penalty at least.

Drill: One on One – Different Scenarios

Skills of beating the keeper can be practised using a straightforward one v one drill. Start from different positions, and allow the striker to run at the keeper, wide or straight, and seek to score. Add a defender and then a support player to develop the drill.

The drill below takes this a step further, to the situation where a team breaks and has an overload. This is a common game situation following a transition of possession, especially from, for example, a corner.

Use With: All ages. Follow offside rules where they apply to the age group.

Objectives: Score in a one v one with a keeper. Create a one v one with the keeper.

Equipment: Balls. Half pitch

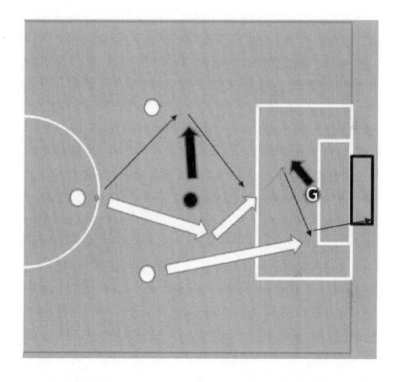

Operation of Drill: This is a three v one game plus a keeper. Play starts in the centre circle. The attacker seeks to draw the defender to make space for a teammate. In the illustration, the defender is drawn wide, the passer runs into the space this defender leaves, draws the keeper and plays across goal to a teammate. But there are many scenarios which will put a player through on the keeper. For example, the player in possession might run at the defender, then slip a pass in behind them to put a teammate through on goal. Allow the strikers to problem solve to create this one-on-one scenario with the keeper.

Key Skills:

- Communication
- Timing of the pass
- Successful completion of the one on one.

Development:

- Add a second defender
- Play a small-sided game with neutrals, who operate with whichever team is in possession. (See diagram below.

The objective of the drill remains the same, to create a one v one scenario with the keeper, and finish this with a goal. The gray players are neutral and work for the team in possession.)

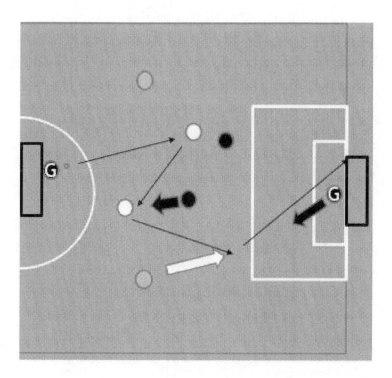

The Ozil Bounce

Mesut Ozil is one of the finest passers of the ball to ever grace this beautiful game. Although, posterity may recall his less for this majestic artistry than for a finish he seems to have developed himself. Known as the Ozil bounce, this clever shot is almost impossible for keepers to read.

Through on goal, one v one, the classy midfielder strikes down on the ball using the instep and drive it into and then off the ground. The ball bounces, but pace is taken off the shot by the downward motion so, although it appears as though the ball will travel low and hard, actually it rises up, and slows. Keepers must commit for the expected shot, only to find the ball lifting over their prostrate bodies, having already launched themselves to the ground.

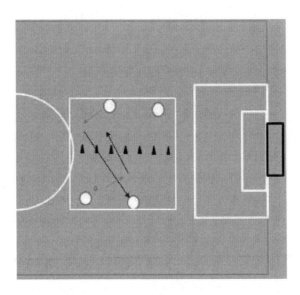

Use with: Under 10s and over. Players must be strong enough to drive the ball into the ground.

Objective: Score by lifting the ball over the keeper, whilst simultaneously taking the pace off the ball.

Equipment: Several low, traffic style, cones. Ball. 10 metres by 10 metres grid.

Operation: Two players either side of the cone 'net. Player one dribbles the ball towards the 'net', plays the Ozil bounce over these cones. The next player controls the ball from the back of the grid and repeats the skill. To produce competition, see how many consecutive successful bounces the players can produce.

Key Skills:

The technique for the bounce is as follows

- Dribble at three quarters to full pace towards the keeper
- Plant the non-kicking foot as though about to let fly with a power shot

- Bend the knee of the shooting foot and lift the foot high
- Bring the shooting foot straight down with force, hitting just below the middle part of the ball
- Use the instep, more towards the heel than the toe, to strike the ball
- The skill works particularly well when running at an angle and shooting at the opposite angle

Development

- Use in a series of one v one run outs against the keeper, allowing the striker to try a variety of finishes

Here are the key points from the chapter:

- Great dribblers are the mavericks of the game
- They must develop their own individuality
- Notwithstanding the above, a good coach will offer dribblers the tools to improve their skills, along with the freedom to exploit them

In the next chapter, look at how the limiting influence of working within a small square can improve touch and finishing.

Finishing Within a Square

'To win you have to score one more goal than your opponent.'
Johan Cruyff.

We will look in this chapter at some finishing drills that can be practised anywhere in the training ground, and which develop the skills of the finisher without always offering the distraction of a physical goal. Some of these drills involve a physical goal, some do not.

Drill: Close Finishing

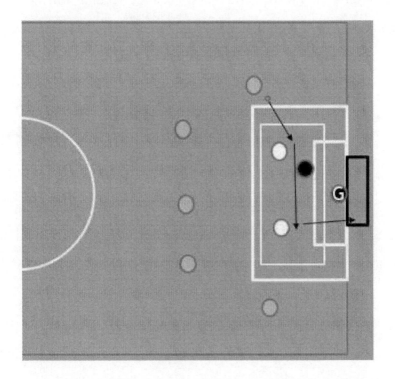

Using a marked out square can help players with positioning
and mimic the pressure of the match situation during drills. Using a
square is particularly helpful with close finishing. And, for all the joy
a 30 yard drive into the top corner brings, far more goals are scored
with a tap in from close range.

Use With: All ages. With young players, the drill may work better by removing the defender and even the second 'finisher'. This creates more space and, consequentially, less pressure. The extra players can be added when the team have mastered the drill.

Objectives: Finish effectively from close range.

Equipment: Balls. Square within the penalty area. The smaller the square, the greater the pressure. As a guide, with an average older youth or adult team, make the square or rectangle slightly smaller than the penalty area.

Operation of Drill: Several feeders are positioned just outside the penalty area. Each has a ball. Inside the square, which is positioned in the penalty area, are two strikers and a defender. The ball is played in to one of the attackers from outside the penalty box. The player must score either by shooting or passing across to their team mate who is in more space. The shot (by either player) must be first time, or after one touch, as in a real game there would be little time to take more than one touch in the box.

Key Skills:

- Communication
- Timing of the pass
- Finishing quickly and efficiently using a side foot shot
- Being aware of chances from rebounds

Development:

- Make the box smaller to add more pressure

Drill: Create Space with Speedy Passing

Some say that this drill was developed by Barcelona specifically for Lionel Messi. Whether that is true, we must draw our own conclusions. Nevertheless, it is a great drill for encouraging movement and injecting pace.

Use With: Talented Under 10s and U11s onwards. There are several stages to the drill, each of which must be completed with precision. Younger players may be too prone to errors, and the drill will then break down, leading to frustrations.

Objectives: Score in a one v one with a keeper. Create a one v one with the keeper.

Equipment: Balls. 5 metre x 5 metre grid, central and bridging the edge of the penalty box. Younger players might benefit from having cones to mark their movements and the direction of their passes.

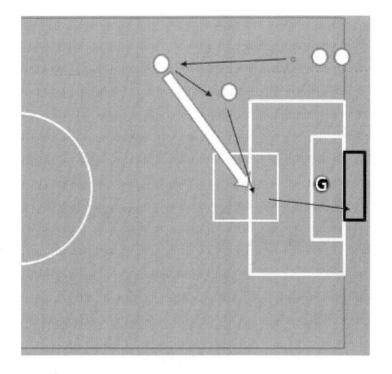

Operation of Drill: Four attackers plus a keeper. The ball starts near the corner, where two players (the passer - Player One and the spare player -Player Four) are lined up. However, the drill can work with players positioned differently. The set up above develops from when a player has reached the by line, then passed backwards at speed, ultimately to exploit space in the central area.

Player One passes firmly backwards to Player Two, who is coming in from off the wing. Player Two plays a wall pass to Player Three, who is positioned close to the corner of the box. Player Two continues their run and receives the return wall pass from Player Three. This is into the marked out shooting square. Player Two shoots first time, or after one touch. (Or, if the coach wished to practise this, Player Two can dribble out of the box and round the keeper.) After each turn players rotate. Player Four becomes Player One, Player One become Player Three, Player Two become Player Four and Player Three becomes Player Two. (Effectively, each player is moving round, geographically, one step).

Key Skills:

- Communication
- Passing firmly and accurately along the ground
- Injecting pace

- Playing and receiving an effective wall pass
- Finishing from the edge of the box

Development:

- Add a defender to operate in the box. Player Two must then use a skill such as a feint or step over to create space for the shot
- Add an extra attacker to attack the far post from a position midway between the corner of the penalty area and the halfway line. This person will need to time their run to offer a passing option or draw the defender away from Player Two. (In the scenario where Player Two plays a pass to this new Player Five, Player Two should continue their run to look for rebounds or a square pass.)

Drill: Sharp Finishing

This is a fast-paced drill which develops neat, one touch finishing from close range. It is a rondo style drill, which means it will encourage touch, awareness and communication.

Use With: Under Nines upwards. Players must be old enough to show anticipation skills.

Objectives: Score in a one touch finish. Get quickly into position for the next finish

Equipment: Balls. Grid 15 metres x 15 metres. (Smaller for more able players, larger for beginners). Cones to make 2-metre-wide gates just outside the perimeter of the square. One gate, or goal, on each side.

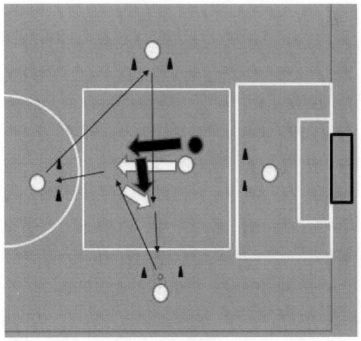

Operation of Drill: One player stands behind each grid. Another remains inside the grid. A defender marks inside the grid. However, this is optional, and for less pressure and to develop more precision in finishing, use the drill without the defender. The ball is played from outside the grid into the player inside the grid. They must finish through a different gate, then move ready for their next finish. Meanwhile, the player whose 'goal' has just be used plays the ball to another player outside the grid. They play the ball into the grid for the striker there to finish in another goal. The striker cannot finish in the goal from where the ball has just been played.

Key Skills:

- Communication
- Timing of the pass
- Anticipation
- One touch, side foot positioning

Development:

- Make inside the grid 2 v 1 to allow more changes of angle in the tight area

Drill: Finish Amongst Chaos

This is a fast-paced drill which mimics the chaotic nature of chances in the box, while providing players with minimal opposition to allow them to perfect their skills.

Use With: Under 11s upwards. Talented younger age groups. Although it is easier than it appears, there is a lot happening in the drill and players must be old enough to focus on their role.

Objectives: Score in a tight space working inside a defender.

Equipment: Balls. 15 metres x 15 metres square. This can be bigger or smaller depending on the ability level of the players. Two goals. Four mannequins placed on the edge of the square, broadly in line with the goal posts

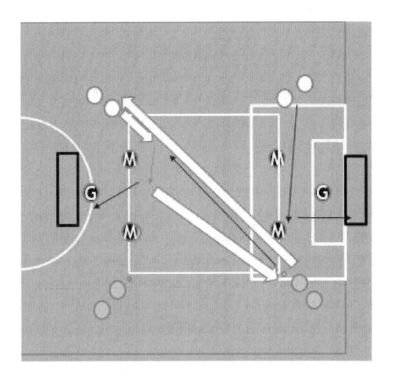

Operation of Drill: Two feeders on each corner of one side of the grid. Two strikers on each corner of opposite sides. The drill works corner to corner, with the feed always coming from the same side.

First feeder passes across the grid. The first attacker in the opposite corner moves forward to meet the ball, drives inside the mannequin and shoots. Meanwhile the same drill is happening in the opposite corners of the square. Further, on finishing the pass for the feed, and on finishing the shot, players cross to the opposite side, changing their role from feeder to shooter and vice versa. Therefore, there is a lot of action occurring inside the square which the striker must put out of his or her mind to concentrate on their touch and shot.

Key Skills:

- Focus and concentration on task; mental strength to put distractions out of the mind
- Communication
- First touch on receiving pass to push ball forward and inside the mannequin defence
- Shooting into corner from a position running parallel with the goal line
- Maintaining accuracy from this shooting position

Development:

- Replace mannequins with real defenders to add pressure onto the shooter.

Here are the key points from the chapter:

- A good coach will be versatile enough to make best use of their resources
- Therefore, not every finishing session needs to take place where the goals are situated

We will look next at the role wide players – wingers, wing backs and full backs – can play in helping to improve finishing.

Crossing and Finishing

'If I feel I'm not influencing games, not scoring goals or making goals, then that's the time I'd pack it in.' Ryan Giggs.

Achieving width is one of the most important offensive philosophies in soccer. Therefore, it is no surprise that denying an opponent width is one of the most common defensive tactics. It follows that the best opportunities wide are both productive, and relatively rare. Teams may be able to put crosses into the box, but often they will be easily cut out. In this chapter we look at drills, strategies and techniques to exploit opportunities when our teams can find some space out wide.

Drill: 2 v 2 + 2

This is a great drill for helping to develop the timing of runs to get onto the end of crosses. It is also fast paced, with an edge of jeopardy. Perfect therefore, especially with younger players.

Use With: Under Nines and over. Players must have the ability to cross a ball.

Objectives: Score following a cross

Equipment: Balls. Enough bibs for five teams of two. Cones to mark out playing area.

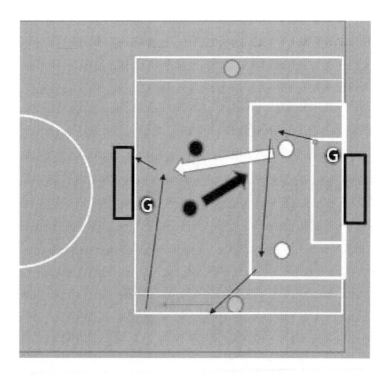

Operation of Drill: A stubby playing area say 25 metres wide by 20 metres long. The extra width is to encourage crosses. However, the actual size can be varied according to the age and skill of the teams.

Each game is two minutes long. At the end of the two minutes teams change as explained below.

Maximum of five teams of two players, although the drill works with three or four teams of two players. Teams begin as follows Team One (attacker), Team Two (defense), Team Three (neutral), then Teams Four and Five are 'next on'. Two goalkeepers are also needed. (Up to four goalkeepers can be used with rotations). Game starts with a pass from a goalkeeper to a teammate from Team One. The two players in that team must work the ball to one of the Team Three players. These players each have a narrow channel on either side of the width of the pitch. Only Team Three can operate in these strips. So, no tackling of these players is allowed. We want them to be able to cross the ball.

A goal is scored when a player scores after a cross. He or she is allowed just one touch before shooting or heading for goal. They may shoot first time. A first-time rebound is also allowed.

If the goal is scored, then Team Two become the attack, Team One defence, and the neutral players in Team Three retain that role.

If an attempt is saved, goes wide, or more touches than are permitted occurs then possession also shifts as above. If the ball goes out of play for any reason, the game restarts as above, with Teams One and Two switching roles.

However, following a cross, a team may simply retain possession, rather than attempt a shot. They are not then allowed to score until a Team Three player has put in another cross.

At full time, the winning team stays on, becoming Team Two (irrespective of whether they were Team One or Two in the previous game). The Neutral Team become Team One, and Team Four becomes Team Three, the Neutral team. Team Five shift up one position to become Team Four. They will be next 'on'. If the result is a draw, then both teams go off. Team Three become Team One, Team Four are Team Two, Team Five become the Neutral Team Three. Team One, who had the advantage of first try in the previous game, drop to Team Five, and Team Two become Team Four. This sounds terribly complicated, so the tables below should help to explain it.

First Game:

Team One	Start with possession/first attackers
Team Two	Start as defence
Team Three	Neutral team providing crosses
Team Four	Will be next on as the Neutral team (unless game results in a draw)
Team Five	Last team to re-join game

If Game 1 results in a victory for Team One

Game Two:

Team One	Now become Team Two
Team Two	Become Team Five
Team Three	Become Team One
Team Four	Become Team Three
Team Five	Become Team Four

If Game 1 results in a victory for Team Two….

Game Two:

Team One	Become Team Five
Team Two	Remain as Team Two
Team Three	Become Team One
Team Four	Become Team Three (Neutral Team)
Team Five	Become Team Four

If Game One is a draw…

Game Two:

Team One	Become Team Five (because they had the first attempt to score in the previous game, which is an advantage)
Team Two	Become Team Four
Team Three	Become Team One
Team Four	Become Team Two
Team Five	Become Team Three

Key Skills:

- Communication
- Getting the ball wide for a cross

- Quality crossing of the pass
- Timing runs to get on the end of crosses
- Finishing first time or with one touch from crosses
- Judging whether to attempt a score or keep possession, depending on the situation of the match

Development:

- The game is quite complicated already, especially if there are five teams. Reducing the size of the goals, or the pitch, adds more pressure and thus develops tighter touch.

Tactic – Dangerous Corners

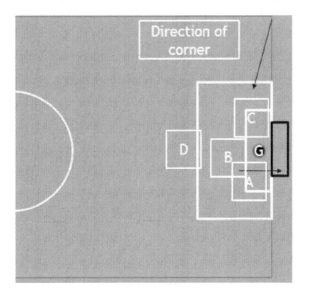

A = Target area for a short corner crossed as an inswinger to the far post

B = Target area for an outswinger

C = Target area for an inswinger

D = Target area for a special leading to a shot from the edge of the box

As we saw earlier, few corners actually result in goals. Sorry to say, but when the crowd roars as their team receive a 92nd minute chance to score an equaliser, their optimism if misplaced. So is the anxiety felt by fans of the team looking to hold onto their lead.

Nevertheless, there are strategies that can be applied. Here we will look at four types of corners and suggest tactics which coaches can employ to maximise their chances of scoring from these. Of course, there is as much controversy about taking corners as there is about defending them. To hear pundits, who presumably know something about the game, bemoaning zonal marking is bizarre, when statistically a combination of zonal and man marking delivers far better results in terms of preventing goals than man marking along. (The figures for man marking against zonal seem to be fairly even.) But we are not as interested in this debate as the other one which surrounds corners: whether short, outswinging or inswinging corners are the most successful.

The answer to that seems to be just about as inconclusive as it is possible to be. A short corner offers the best chance of retaining possession, which will in turn offer the most likely opportunity for a goal scoring chance, while reducing the risk of conceding on the break.

135

An outswinger seems logically to be a waste of the opportunity, since the ball is heading away from goal, and so scoring is far harder. However, as we shall see, there are a number of misnomers here, since statistically the greatest number of chances fall from outswinging corners. Yet bizarrely the fan's favourite, the inswinger, delivers the most goals, but the fewest chances. This suggests that an inswinger is mostly likely to bring about a goal, whilst it is also the most likely to result in the keeper catching the ball and launching a rapid counter attack.

The best option, therefore, seems to be to offer a series of different corners, outswinging, inswinging and short, in order to cause most doubt in the minds of the defense. The process can be made even more complex by adding a 'special' to a team's arsenal. We offer a drill to practise one of these as well.

Tactic and Drill: The Short Corner

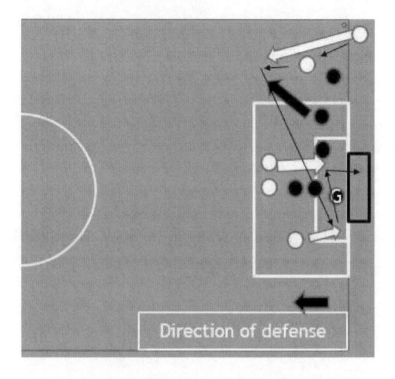

Direction of defense

There are a couple of principles underlying the short corner; firstly, it either creates an overlap and a two v one situation, or a second defender is forced out from the defense creating more space in the box. Both are advantageous to the attack. As explained earlier, it does allow the option to keep possession, which can be useful towards the end of a game when a lead is being protected. The tactic here allows for a deep, inswinging cross, with the attack looking to head the ball back across the goal. The drill which follows helps to create the space for the cross, or the 2 v 1 overlap.

Use With: Under 10s upwards. Younger if the ability is there to cross the ball.

Objectives: Achieve either a two v one overlap, or cross from a more favourable angle.

Equipment: Balls. Cones to represent a half a goal. Grid 20 metres wide by 10 metres deep.

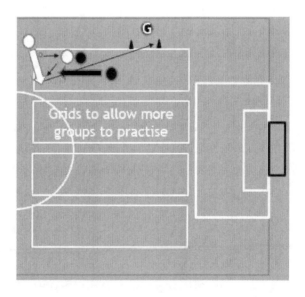

Operation of Drill: Two attackers versus two defenders and a goalkeeper. One striker takes the corner, the other stands three to five metres in. One defender marks this striker but must be behind him due to distance rules from corners. The other defender covers midway in the grid.

The corner is played short and firm. The taker immediately runs towards the back of the grid, at a slight angle. The receiving attacker makes a decision – whether to turn his or her marker, and head on goal, or lay an instant pass back towards his partner on the edge of the grid. Usually, this will be the option. The spare defender will attempt to close down the corner taker and prevent the deep cross from this favourable angle. The corner taker aims for the twin cones, representing the target area for a deep cross. The goalkeeper stands behind the cones. Their job is simply to field the ball. Swap roles regularly.

Key Skills:

- Communication
- Accurate, one touch passing

- Decision making as to what represents the best opportunity for an attack on goal
- Ability to lift a deep, inswinging cross, with the instep/toes. The player strikes with the opposite foot to the side they are on, so right footer from the left, left footer from the right
  - Arms for balance
  - Plant the non-kicking foot
  - Strike low down on the ball using the front of the instep in the big toe area
  - Follow through smoothly

Development:

- Add more players and operate on pitch

Tactic and Drill: The Outswinger

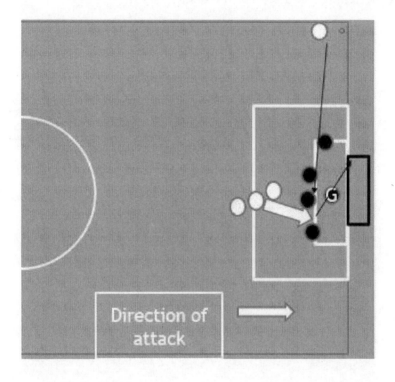

Direction of attack

An outswinger comes when the player taking the corner strikes with the same foot as the side they are on. So, left footer from the left side, right footer from the right side. The ball draws away from the keeper, making it difficult for them to catch the cross. Since the target area is larger (see diagrams) than for an inswinger, it is easier to miss out the man on the front post. However, good contact is needed in winning the header, as the ball must be directed on target.

141

Headers which go back across the goal in the direction from which the corner came are often the most successful.

Drill

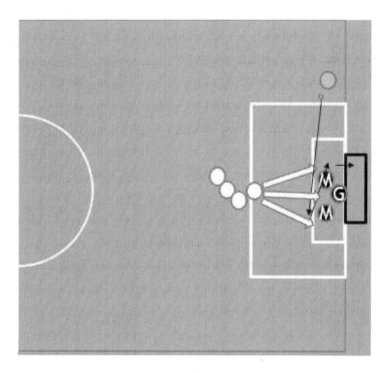

Use With: Under 12 upwards (both for the drill and for an in-match tactic). The players must be able to cross from the corner and be able and permitted to head the ball back. Whether heading is allowed with younger players will depend on the rules in local leagues and football associations.

Objectives: Protect the far post runner from the defence to give space for a free header.

Equipment: Balls. Mannequins to act as defenders. It is too great a risk to use a real defence as there will be a possibility of head injury, which must be avoided.

Operation of Drill: Four attackers line up close together between the penalty spot and the edge of the area. There must not be space for a defender to get between them. A feeder will lob balls into the box (reducing impact risks which come from a kicked cross), aiming for the far post approximately eight to ten metres from the goal. The strikers will break near post (first attacker), Centre goal (middle attacker), far post for the third attacker and the rear most striker remains still, for rebounds.

Thus, the middle two attackers are thereby protected from the defence by their teammates, giving them a better chance of a clear run. The third placed attacker is the best protected, and it is he or she who is intended to get onto the ball. The feeder aims for the far post, and the striker aims to head the ball either back across goal, or to their far corner for a direct score.

Key Skills:

- Communication
- Discipline to follow set role
- Ability to head cleanly
- Awareness of the second ball

Development:

- As the drill develops, and players try different positions, it will be clear who is the best far post header of the ball.
- A game of bulldog using the same positions (but no ball) can be played. Use rugby tackle tags to avoid injury. Real defenders now replace the mannequins. Play the game whereby on the whistle, the attacking players try to reach the goal line in their set positions, and the defenders try to tear off their Velcro tags.

Through doing this the coach will work out who is the best at avoiding tackles.

- By combining the information from these tests, it should be apparent which players go where for this outswinger corner tactic

Tactic and Drill: The Inswinger

A perfectly placed inswinging corner is almost impossible to defend against. A poor corner of this kind will be cut out by the near post defender, go straight out of play or be easily caught by the keeper.

The near post flick is the best inswinging corner.

Use With: Under 12s upwards. Provide a feeder to lob the ball for accuracy if the kicker cannot deliver with precision. For heavier practice, use only with adults. In any case, do not overuse.

Objectives: Deliver a corner to the near post for the flick on

Equipment: Balls.

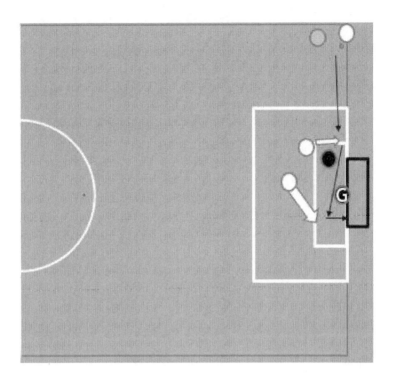

Operation of Drill: Feeder/corner taker takes the inswinging corner. The first attacker moves from the corner of the six-yard box towards the bye line for the flick on. He or she runs in front of the defender. Often, the ball will flick off the defender's head. That is fine, the result is the same. The second striker attacks the far post. Flick on corners often go straight into the net.

Key Skills:

- Precision in delivery of the corner
- Confidence to allow the ball to flick off the head
- Striker looking alert for the flick on

Development:

- Because of head injury and concussion concerns, we should not overplay this move in drills.

Tactic and Drill: A Special Move

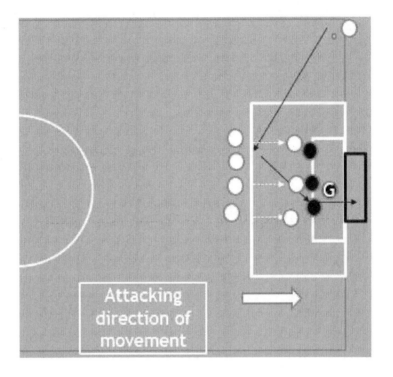

Used sparingly, the pulled back corner is highly effective. It must, however, have a surprise value as teams will quickly spot the plan and nullify it if they are expecting it. Losing possession on the edge of the box when the team has advanced for a corner leaves a side susceptible to the counterattack!

Use With: All ages

Objectives: Create a goal scoring opportunity by fooling the defence

Equipment: Balls.

Operation of Drill: Corner, with a line of strikers on the edge of the box, and a line of defence marking zonally.

As the run up is taken for the corner, the attackers move in towards the goal, so it looks as though the corner will be a normal one. A player remains of the edge of the box. The corner is played low and hard to this player who takes a touch and shoots or shoots first time. The best shot will be hard and low, as with so many players in the box the keeper will be unsighted, and there is a strong possibility of a deflection which will, with luck, go into the net.

Key Skills:

- Ability to disguise the pass by running up as if taking a normal corner
- Discipline to do your job
- Ability to strike a ball moving across the body cleanly, low and hard.

- Good shooting technique
- Awareness of rebounds

Development:

- Play a corner competition. Two teams of five. Goalkeeper can play for both teams. Five corners each, one per player. Five points for a goal, three points for an attempt on target, one point for an attempt on goal.

As the game evolves, and different tactics come into vogue, the role of the full back changes. Sometimes, the position has defence as its primary concern. This is often the case in a back four. However, the modern game sees wing backs (the wide defenders in a five) providing width for teams operating with narrower midfields and forward lines. These wing backs, as the name suggests, have a dual role which involves a significant attacking input.

Therefore, the modern wide defender (for want of a better name) must be comfortable on the ball, have pace, be fit enough to get up and down the wing, have some dribbling skills and be able to cross.

These defenders should take part in all attack-based drills, and work on their dribbling and crossing skills. Take Achraf Hamini; the Inter wing back directly contributed to sixteen goals (seven scored and nine assists) in just 33 games in the 2020-21 season. Meanwhile, the twin threats of Andy Robinson and Trent Alexander Arnold at Liverpool have helped to make the team possibly Europe's strongest.

Drill: The Overlapping full back (or Wing Back)

This drill will help teams get their full backs forward.

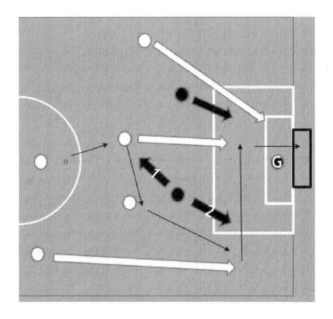

Use With: Under 9s upwards. The drill is a rondo drill, and therefore players have minimal pressure. Younger players will achieve enough success with the drill to make it worthwhile.

Objectives: Draw the defence infield then shift the ball wide quickly. Cross accurately and finish the chance.

Equipment: Balls. Half a pitch

Operation of Drill: This is a five v two rondo, plus a keeper, played in half a pitch. The drill can vary as it is played, provided the principles are maintained. The ball begins in the centre circle. The full back or wing back starts deep. The ball is played into central midfield, on the further side to the space into which the wing back will run.

A player remains wide on the opposite flank, further advanced than the wing back, to occupy a defender. (If during the drill, this player is left unmarked, the pass can simply be played to them, and they operate as the player who will ultimately cross the ball!).

The second pass is short and injects pace into the attack. The third pass is the decisive one, hit wide and into space for the wing back to run onto. By now the defence is stretched. Strikers now make their runs into the box. The wing back crosses and the strikers attempt to finish.

Key Skills:

- Communication
- Injecting pace when space is created
- Precision one and two touch passing
- Quality crossing, firm and away from the keeper

Development:

- Allow the rondo to develop freely, giving players problem solving opportunities
- Add a further defensive player to narrow space

<u>Here are the key points from the chapter</u>:

- Exploiting wide possession involves teaching players how to make effective runs
- Working on corners is an important coaching strategy, but not an essential one

Next, we will consider the unusual, spectacular and frankly jaw dropping.

One Touch and Other Special Finishes

'When I was younger, I used to visualise myself scoring wonder goals, stuff like that.' Wayne Rooney.

Do we play soccer to enjoy ourselves, or to win? Hopefully, both, but surely the former is the more important? Which leads us to this chapter. Spectacular goals stick in the memory but are actually very rare. Gareth Bale's splendid overhead kick in the Champions League final where his Real Madrid side beat Liverpool comes to mind. Maradona's incredible dribble in the 'Hand of God' World Cup quarter final also.

But most players will score, at best, just a couple of super-spectacular finishes in their entire playing career. Does that negate us trying them? Definitely not. And if we are prepared to try the out of this world, then surely, we must practise for this? Point made. Because, it is hard to think of anything more enjoyable than flying through the air, head horizontal, back to goal, and connecting with the knee high cross that is just behind us.

It's fun. Kids love to try the impossible. And so do adults.

However, this is a serious book, so let us start with a couple of special finishes that do lead to their fair share of goals. Before we delve into the land of dreams, of course.

Drill: Turn and Shoot

A very true to life drill. Often a striker will be in a position close to the edge of the box, with their back to goal. There may not be a good passing option, and the best choice will be to turn and shoot.

Use With: All ages.

Objectives: Perfect the half turn in both directions and deliver a powerful and accurate shot.

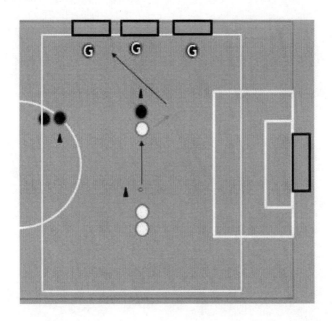

Equipment: Several balls. Three small goals. Three cones marking: attacker line, defence line, receiving position. Playing area approximately 30 metres long by 20 metres wide.

Operation of Drill: A player moves from the attacker line to the receiving cone. Meanwhile, a defender moves from the defence line and lines up close behind the attacker. The next attacker passes the ball firmly into the feet of the attacker who will shoot. The attacker receives the pass on the half turn, creates space with the turn and shoots at one of the three goals. The drill also works with one full size goal as a target, but as good coaches wish to encourage success, it is better to use three goals, which increases the chances of scoring.

After each go, the attacker joins the back of the defence line and vice versa.

Key Skills:

- Receiving the ball on the half turn
  - Position the chest approximately 45 degrees to the pass
  - Keep the arms out for balance or protection
- Control the ball
  - With the outside of the foot, shifting it wide and presenting the chance to shoot with the opposite foot
  - With the outside of the foot, then pulling the ball back 180 degrees to allow space for a shot with the controlling foot
    - Dip the shoulder to feint when dragging the ball back

- With the instep of the rear foot, committing the defender's weight forward and allowing either an immediate shot with the other foot, or a second touch to create more space
- With a particular skill, such as a drag back or feint, which may wrong foot the defender creating more space
- 'Feel' the position of the defender using the arms or buttocks
- Shoot after one or two touches
  - Use the arms for balance and protection
  - Drive with the laces
  - If enough time and space, use the instep for accuracy

Development:

- Change the angle of the pass
- Add in a second defender
- Try harder to control passes, such as at knee or chest height

Drill: Developing the Near Post Flick

Another important but everyday finish next. This is a very useful finishing technique to possess. We also see in this drill how a coach might build up technique and skill level with various developmental stages. The finish simply involves a deviation of the ball. The pace to beat the keeper comes from the pace on the cross. The keeper will be drawn to their near post as the attacker makes their run across it. This means they have little time to readjust if the flick heads towards their far post. Equally, if the flick targets the near post, there is little reaction time available to the goalkeeper due to the close proximity of the goal to the striker. In addition, if the keeper does save the flick, they are unlikely to hold on to the ball, presenting a scoring opportunity from the rebound. Finally, there is a strong possibility of a deflection off a defender.

The biggest challenge when operating the drill with younger players is to encourage the passer to pull their cross away from the goal (making it harder for the keeper to intercept). Young players tend to aim their crosses towards the goal and will need to practise in order to pull the ball back consistently.

Use With: All ages.

Objectives: Flick the ball first time with the outside of the boot.

Equipment: Several balls. Goal. Younger players will find cones helpful for showing them where to make their runs and from where to deliver their cross. This is especially true as the drill develops.

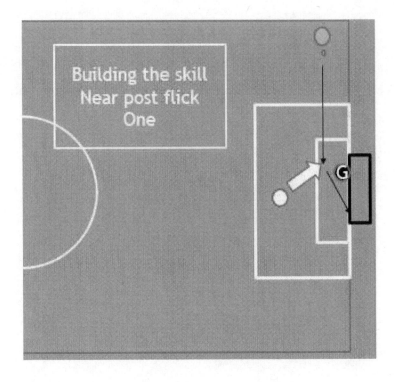

Operation of Drill:

Pass from the by-line. Attacker runs in at an angle and flicks the ball with the outside of their boot, from outside the near post, aiming for the far post.

Key Skills:

- Timing the run
- Having the confidence to allow the ball to hit the outstretched foot, rather than seeking to shoot explicitly

Development 1:

- Player dribbles and crosses
- Add a mannequin or cone to dribble around.

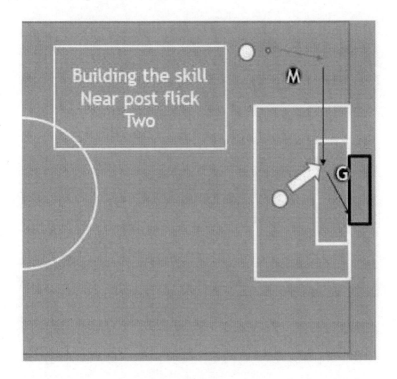

Building the skill
Near post flick
Two

Development 2:

- Making an angled run

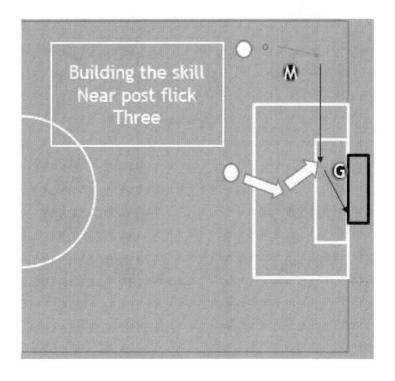

Development 3:

- Adding a defender

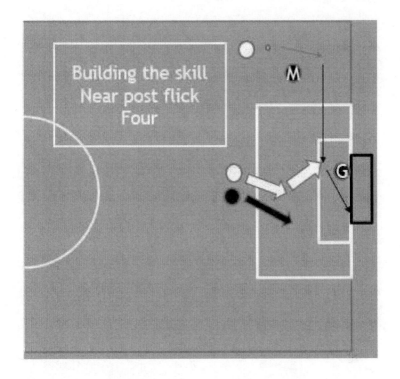

Development 4:

- Adding a support player

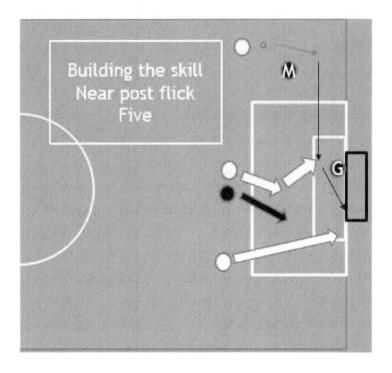

Development 5:

- Match play drill
- Six v four plus a keeper rondo attack v defence on half a pitch. Get the ball wide to create space for the player to attack the near post for the flick.

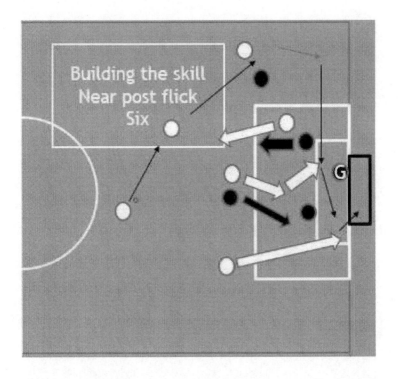

Building the skill
Near post flick
Six

The principles behind the development of drills to this final, match play situation, can be applied to many of the drills we suggest in this book. Clearly, here we start from the beginning with a drill for young players who are just beginning to learn about tactical plays. A coach of, say, an Under 12 team may begin by including a defender, and develop from there. When running an adult team, we may reinforce the skills with all players to refocus, and quickly move onto a match play drill.

Drill: The Overhead Kick

Time for some fun...

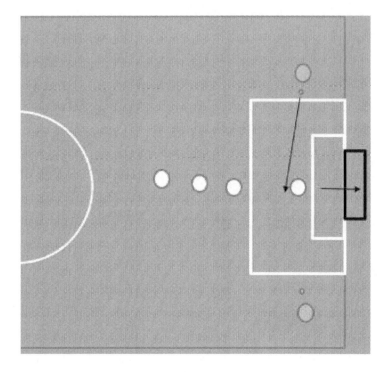

The thrill here comes from the skill rather than the drill. It is because players, especially younger ones, will love the action, the coach can use the drill to concentrate on technique.

Use With: As young as have the coordination to work through the moves. Under 10s, certainly. Perhaps younger. Whilst coaches will want to avoid the frustration of constant failure, they know their players and their capabilities.

Objectives: Complete an overhead kick.

Equipment: Balls. Goal.

Operation of Drill: Two feeders on opposite sides of the penalty area. Balls lobbed sympathetically into the box. Players stand with their back to goal and attempt an overhead kick. Give each player an attempt from each side. Players will enjoy watching their peers, so the normal rule of action, action, action can be suspended here.

Key Skills:

- Watch the ball throughout
- Jump, leading with the non-kicking foot to generate height
- Fall backwards, watching the ball throughout

- The non-kicking foot will naturally begin to lift as the head and back fall towards the ground. Probably, the kicking foot will remain on the ground at this stage
- Judge when the ball enters the kicking range
- Bring the kicking foot up towards the ball
- There is no need to kick the ball hard. Both its and the players momentum will generate force
- As the kicking foot rises, the non-kicking leg drops
- The upper body should be close to horizontal at the point of impact
- Control your descent. Twist to land on the side rather than back, and break the fall with the hand and legs
- Landing on the elbow, head or shoulder should be avoided, as this can lead to injury

Development:

- Try crosses from different angles, heights and speeds. When players become highly skilled kicked crosses can be introduced. However, bear in mind that even top professionals fail at this skill more than they succeed, and constant failure can be discouraging.

- Add a goalkeeper.
- (Avoid adding a defender, as there is a risk of injury if they get too close, both to the defender and the attacker if they are tackled in mid-air!)

Drill: The Scissor Kick

To clarify, we are talking here about a corkscrew kick. In some areas, the overhead kick is also known as the scissor kick. The drill set up is much as above, so please follow the diagram for the overhead kick as a guide on which to base this drill.

Use With: Under 10s upwards. The technique for the scissor kick is a little easier as the non-kicking foot can remain planted.

Objectives: Complete a scissor kick accurately.

Equipment: Balls.

Operation of Drill: Two feeders, one on each side of the penalty area, broadly in line with the penalty spot. The striker stands chest on to the feeder, broadly on the penalty spot. The feeder lobs the ball in, and the striker executes a scissor kick. Vary the side from which the ball is delivered.

Key Skills:

- Watch the ball throughout
- Move to position yourself slightly behind the line of the ball. We are aiming to contact the ball just in front of the line of the body
- Move to judge the trajectory of the ball. Ideally, contact is achieved at between knee and thigh height
- Put the arms out and rotate them back so they are twisted in a straight line towards the ball. The arm on the side of the kicking foot is furthest from the ball
- As the ball approaches, rotate the arms like a corkscrew, while simultaneously rotating the kicking foot towards the ball. The kicking foot is the one furthest from goal.
- Drop hips and keep head over the ball
- Using the instep will give more chance of making contact with the ball but is more effective with crossing rather than shooting. Aim for contact with the laces for a shot

- Power will come from the momentum of the ball and the rotation of the body, so there is no need to impart too much whip on the ball

Development:

- Change the angles, height and power of the feed
- As players become more expert, bring in crosses with the foot rather than feeds with the hands.

Tactic: Arriving late from Midfield

The hardest player for an organised defence to pick up is a midfielder arriving late. Such players are often tracked by their opposite number from the midfield; however, sometimes the tracking is lost as the attacking midfielder runs past their opponent.

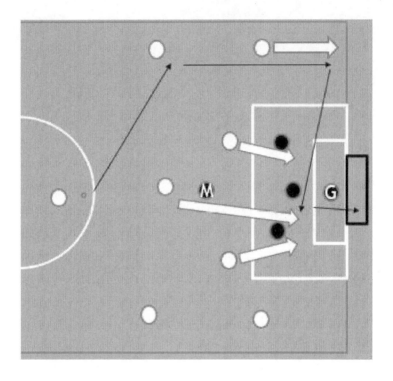

Use With: Under 9s upwards. The concept of attacking from deep is a key one for successful soccer. It should be installed in players as early as possible.

Objectives: Arrive late to finish.

Equipment: Balls. Half pitch. Goal. Mannequin to act as the defender the midfielder will run past. (This can be an active defender when working with older and more experienced players.)

Operation of Drill: Seven versus three and a keeper, or four and a keeper if no mannequin is used. Players line up broadly as per diagram, paying attention to offside (from U13 level, or wherever the league in which your team plays introduce this law). The ball is shifted quickly wide and then forward giving the winger a pass onto which they can run. Two attackers make their run, near post and far post, occupying two of the three deepest defenders. The midfielder who will go on to score runs past their mannequin (or defender), and into the box centrally. They angle their run to find space around the spare defender. The cross comes in, usually pulled slightly back behind the near post runner, taking the two nearest defenders out of the game. The midfielder arrives and finishes with a side foot shot. Their momentum, and that of the ball, will generate power, and as they will be arriving at full speed, an instep shot, head over the ball, will ensure control.

Key Skills:

- Timing of run
- Communication
- Using speed to avoid defence
- Controlled finish

- Crosser taking time to look up before cross, to anticipate position of arriving midfielder
- Crosser able to deliver a controlled, accurate and sympathetic cross

Development:

- Play a six a side game. Two midfielders on each team wear a bib. Only these players can score.
- Only goals scored from a deep run count.

Drill: Opening the body for the Curler

It is the perfect finish. The French and Arsenal striker, Thierry Henry, was the master, but we see it regularly scored at the highest level. The pacy striker breaks from wide and cuts inside, outpacing his marker. He leans slightly away from the ball, and strokes it, without breaking stride, towards the outside of the far post.

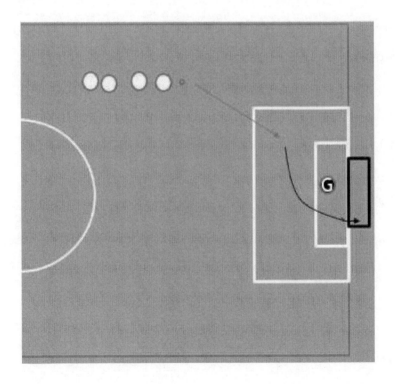

The advancing keeper has no chance so far out of his reach is the ball, yet it does not matter, because the shot is going wide. But…that attempt was hit with the instep of the inner foot, not too firmly, the player's momentum injecting pace. By leaning very slightly away, the foot imparts spin. The ball comes back towards the goal and nestles inside the side netting of the far post.

Use With: Under 11s upwards. The skill is difficult, because younger players will find it hard to visualise the curve of the ball and will try to shoot too hard.

Objectives: Score with a curving shot inside the far post

Equipment: Strikers and a keeper, balls.

Operation of Drill: Start wide between the halfway line and edge of the penalty area. Drive at pace towards the corner of the box. Enter the penalty box and shoot as per above.

Key Skills:

- Run at pace

- Body position
- Confidence to stroke the ball with the instep, rather than shoot with power

Development:

- Add a defender. This player should defend from the outside of the striker.
- Now allow the defender to work between the player and the goal, which will force the striker to cut inside to get the shot away.

Drill: Lob Tennis

There is something very pleasing about a lob. It is becoming an even more useful weapon as keepers adapt to be more like outfield players. Their starting position is often further forwards than in the past, making them vulnerable to this skill. Also, when they advance to be the extra player, if their pass is misplaced, or its target fails to control the ball, again a clever striker can nip in to try a long-distance lob.

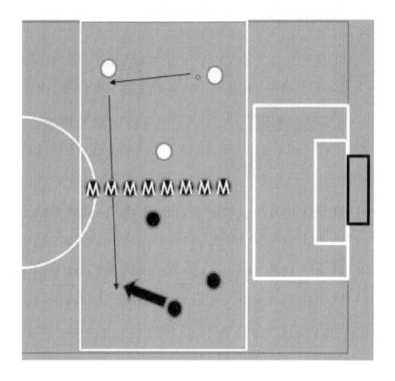

Use With: Under 11s upwards. Players must be tall enough to be able to control a bouncing ball

Objectives: Win a point 'tennis style' by playing an accurate lob.

Equipment: Grid approximate 25 metres long by 15 metres wide, subject to age range. Row of tall cones or mannequins to act as a net. Or, if available, play with a soft ball (to control bounce) on a regular tennis court.

Operation of Drill: Three, four or five a side depending on the age of players and size of the area available. Play like tennis. Player serves by dropping the ball from hands and volleying over the net. With more able players, a 'service box' can be laid out with cones. The receiving team has five touches to return the ball with a lob. They may use any part of the body legal in soccer to control the ball – head, chest, legs, feet etc. They may play the ball in any way they wish during their up to five touches, including passing along the ground. However, the return over the 'net' must be a lob.

A point is won either when the opposition cannot return the ball within their five touches, or when the opposition return the ball, but it lands out of play.

An interesting variation which leads to longer rallies is to allow a player to be a goalkeeper. They may catch the ball from serve or use their hands in any way they wish. However, they must pass the ball next, in any way legal for a keeper. They may not throw the ball back over the 'net', nor lob the ball over with their next touch.

Key Skills:

- Eyes on the ball
- Move body into position as early as possible, judging the trajectory of the ball
  - Arms out for balance
  - Place non-kicking foot beside where the ball will be struck
  - Strike the ball as close to about six inches from the ground as it is possible to do. The higher the bounce, the harder the skill (Note: it is not possible to lob a ball that is on the ground. It can be chipped, or it can be flicked with the toes, but not lobbed)
  - Bring the kicking leg back thirty to forty five degrees
  - Bring the foot through smoothly, watching the ball and maintaining wide arms for balance
  - Hit the ball low down, using the instep
  - Point the toes down
  - Lean slightly back to get height
  - Follow through smoothly

Development:

- Add in a driven lob using the laces
- Hit directly through the ball, with a firm follow through
- Encourage players to hit across the ball to learn about inducing swerve

<u>Here are the key points from the chapter</u>:

- We return to our conclusions from the chapter on volleying. Spectacular finishes are rare but offer value in that they are fun to practise. Fun is what soccer is about. A player who enjoys themselves in training (and matches) will become a better all-round player
- By using drills to practise complex skills and techniques, players' general coordination will improve, especially younger ones
- In this chapter we have seen an example of how a coach can build up drills to develop a skill or tactic

Close to thirty per cent of goals come from set pieces. Many of these from penalties. The spot kick is the focus of our next chapter.

Penalties, and Penalty Shoot Outs

'Scoring goals is a great feeling, but the most important thing to me is that the team is successful. It doesn't matter who scores the goals as long as we're winning.' Cristiano Ronaldo.

Here's an interesting fact. If a player takes a good penalty, the keeper cannot save it. Note, not might not, or even probably won't, but physically is unable to stop that penalty. There are a lot of very clever people who spend a lot of very valuable time studying things that are both extremely obvious, and not terribly important. Not in the scheme of things. We might argue that this is one of them.

Still, that their findings are nevertheless interesting cannot be denied. To take the question in hand, it has been proven that a well hit shot enters the goal before has had time to move. In fact, the ball is pretty much past the poor old keeper before they have had much in the way of time to even react.

Yet one in four penalties does not result in a goal. In fact, just over that figure. These are either penalties that are saved or miss the target. So, what goes wrong on these occasions? Or right, for the keeper at least? The second question is the easier of the two to answer. A professional keeper is able to study the actions of the taker, to know where statistically they are likely to place the ball. That is not something we are likely to be able to do at amateur or youth level. A professional keeper might make a marginal gain by working on their reaction times. But in all honesty, it seems as though there is still not much they can do to alter the outcome of the penalty. If they guess right, and the penalty lands within their sphere of coverage, they will probably save it; if they guess wrong a goal will most likely be scored. If they face a good penalty, then they would be better having a cup of tea and a sandwich than trying to prevent the goal. (A sort of unexpected not-half-time-break.)

Therefore, we are left to conclude that if the penalty taker can get it right, then they will score. That 25% of penalties that are missed are examples of the penalty taker getting it wrong. So, the aim of this chapter is to give our players the best chance of getting it right. The same rules apply whether we are facing the drama of a penalty shoot-out, taking a last-minute spot kick when we are 1-0 down, or we've already got the game won, and the pressure on the kick is minimal.

Other than for our player's personal pride.

It makes sense, then, to regard all penalties as being ones to decide the outcome of the world cup. If we can prepare for that situation, we will be fine taking a penalty when we are 5-0 up in a pre-season friendly.

Let's us begin by analysing the perfect penalty, then look at how we can have the best chance of delivering such a shot. Because, we'll say it again, if the penalty is good, it will result in a goal.

Fact: Power counts

Again, we need to rely on research as we look at the power factor. It seems pretty clear that hitting the ball hard is important. We might watch players like Bruno Fernandes, with his little skip and stroke in the run up and think that it looks highly impressive. The secret there, though, is that Fernandes (and others like him) are not so much great penalty takers, as extremely fast processors of information. Because, they are able to see the minutest movement in the keeper that their skip – a hesitation by any other name – brings about, and adjust their body quickly to place the ball where the keeper is not.

Watch a few penalties from players such as these, and notice how often their shot is extremely saveable, other than for the fact the keeper has already committed. In fact, statistically, only about half of gently hit penalties result in goals. Of course, in contrast, accuracy is good. It is highly unlikely that a soft penalty will miss the target, but the keeper will save it if they guess right.

Hitting the ball as hard as possible is a better option. But not the best. While keepers rarely save a powerful penalty, a thunderbolt has a high – about 30% - chance of missing the target. And if those are the figures at professional level, then it is fair to assume that amateurs and youth players will miss on even more occasions.

Statistically, the best strength for a penalty lies at about seventy five percent of full power, suggesting that a combination of speed and accuracy will result in a goal. Indeed, there is about a ninety per cent chance of success with a well-directed (as opposed to 'perfectly' directed) penalty hit with three quarters force.

Fact: Placement Counts

Well, obviously. Hit the ball in the corner and you are going to score. Hit it straight at the keeper and you will not. Except, it's not quite as simple as that. Because statistically there are three points where a goal is most likely to occur. The two bottom corners, because the keeper simply cannot get there. And the middle of the goal. Where the keeper stands.

So perhaps we should encourage our players to aim for the middle. After all, there is almost no chance of missing the target then. Except, of course, the middle of the goal works because it is the last place a keeper expects the penalty to be hit. As soon as they spot a pattern and expect the penalty to be aimed straight at them, or at least, straight at where they were a millisecond before, they will just remain upright and save the shot.

Maybe, therefore, there is a value in the third or fourth penalty taker aiming one straight, as long as the other penalties have been traditionally hit to the corners. But on the whole, such a tactic will only work where there is an element of surprise about it. (Having said this, we are surprised that keepers do not stay upright more often to takers such as Fernandes, who nearly always adopt their 'skip' approach. After all, he is hitting the ball effectively from a standing start and will not be able to impart much pace. Unless a softly hit shot is right in the corner, the keeper will have a decent chance of stopping it.)

The most certain spot to score is in the top corner, where a goal is guaranteed. Except…to generate the power to lift the ball here is difficult. While the keeper rarely makes a stop, gravity, physics and fine detail come to his or her aid, and there is a good chance the ball will miss its target. Better then to still hit the corner, **but a controlled shot to the bottom corner is the best place for a penalty**.

The Mental Side of the Game

It seems straightforward. A penalty is only twelve yards from goal. The goal is eight yards wide. Anything hit with even three quarters power within a yard inside of either post will score. Most half decent amateur players could hit a target that big from just twelve yards away.

But in the match situation, something happens. Doubts creep in. 'Has the keeper guessed which way I'll hit the ball?' 'Shall I aim just a bit more centrally just to be safe?' 'What if the keeper goes early? I'll hit it a bit harder, just to be sure...' Or, the worst of all, we decide to change our aim as we run up to strike the ball. Our body position, so carefully nurtured, deserts us, and the ball flies wide.

We can address this. In fact, more easily than a professional. Because nobody is going to be analysing our players', or our own, penalty taking technique. Not at the level at which we are playing.

Let us start with those doubts...

'Has the keeper guessed which way I'll hit the ball?' So what? Our penalty will be in the corner.

'Shall I aim just a bit more centrally just to be safe?' Why? We've hit this penalty a thousand times in training. It always works. It will now.

'What if the keeper goes early?' Again, it doesn't matter. Because they are going to have to go extremely early to save our shot. And surely, the referee will spot that, and order a retake. Frankly, if they don't, and the keeper transgresses that blatantly, then it is out of our control. We only consider that which we can control.

And if we change our mind during the run up, then the coach has made a huge mistake in asking us to take a spot kick…

Practice

So, we practice. Firstly, without a keeper. We follow the same routine every time. Once we have this perfected, and can hit the same spot every time, then we can introduce a keeper. And practice some more. Until when the point comes in the 87th minute of the game, and we must score to go top of the league, or lift the trophy, our muscle memory takes over, and we run through the same routine we always do. With the same outcome. Success.

Technique: The perfect penalty…a thousand times over

Our penalty technique is what works for us. If we are good enough to hit a top corner a hundred times out of a hundred, then that's where we aim. (Remembering to book the flight to Spain so we can sign up with Barcelona...) More likely, we are going to hit the bottom corner. A shot along the ground requires less power than a blast into the top corner and is therefore more likely to result in success.

We work out what delivers the outcome we want for us. That is what we practise. Every training session. Every week. It is then what we use in the match. Every time. It is us against the keeper, and almost every bullet is loaded into our gun. Our opponent has only one. A not very good one at that. His only hope is that we will make a mistake.

Here is a system that will work for many. Use it, try it, adapt it.

- Place the ball yourself on the penalty spot to ensure confidence that it is not in a divot
- Walk away.
- Take five deep breaths, exhaling slowly, to settle heart rate

- Meanwhile, visualise the penalty: the strike, where it will hit, the net bulging. Try not to look at the corner at which you are aiming. If it helps to look, glance at some other spots as well, to confuse the keeper
- Have a run up of at least six yards.
- An angle of forty-five degrees seems, statistically, to be best
- Strike the ball with the instep
- The goal will not move, so keep your eye on the ball. That way, the keeper's movements will not distract either
- Strike through the ball using the exact technique used in every practice.
- Celebrate…we have scored.

Here are the key points from the chapter:

- There is a science behind penalties
- Techniques, skills, statistics and mindset each plays a part in a successful penalty
- Practice is therefore important

If percentage wise, penalties are the most successful set piece, then second (a distant second) are direct free kicks in the attacking third.

Free Kicks

'I love scoring goals for England and playing for England. That's one of the reasons I didn't retire.' David Beckham.

It is interesting to see how the free kick has developed. It really isn't very long ago that any free kick from mid-way inside a team's own half forwards resulted in the big men heading upfield. The ball would be lumped high and long and in the ensuing battle, the attacking side would hope that their route one tactic paid dividends.

Usually, it didn't. Often, with the defence pushed up, such a manoeuvre resulted in a fast counterattack. An attacking position of barely moderate interest turned into a defensive one of much threat.

In fact, such an approach seemed typically British. Perhaps it was the poor playing surfaces that put a hold on coaches building from the back. Now that even semi pros play on carpets, and a Sunday League side in the park can count on something that is at least green (as opposed to the rutted brown of not many years ago), the long hoik upfield is, thankfully, a thing consigned almost totally to the coaching bin.

Nowadays, a free kick is taken quickly, possession maintained, and seen as a disadvantage to the attacking side, at least compared to the position they were previously in. A break in their fluidity. Which is why, of course, defences are so happy to give away a free kick.

This changes in the attacking third. Most teams have a couple of free kick specialists. Wide free kicks which result in a cross lead to goals nearly four per cent of the time, better than the return for corners. Shots, meanwhile, have double the success of corners when it comes to goals. At 6.3% success for the taker (deflections and own goals improve the ratio) a free kick is not as valuable as a penalty, or a two on one break, but it is still enough to be a significant factor in a coach's planning.

Therefore, in this chapter, we will break down some of the most successful methods of taking an attacking free kick.

Drills

There are not many ways of practising direct shot drills to involve several players. The best approach is to send off the specialist free kick takers to train at one end of the pitch. The generic drill below offers five different shooting positions and involves a host of mannequins to act as a wall from different positions.

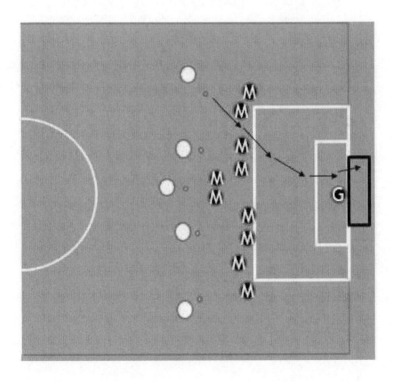

Technique: The Power Shot

Cristiano Ronaldo made this free kick his own, and now it is usual practice to see players examining the ball carefully before placing it for their kick. The secret to Ronaldo's driven shot, one which dips and curves, is to strike the hard area around the air valve of the ball. Making contact here causes the ball to perform acrobatics in the air, making the kick much harder for keepers to judge.

- Place ball for the kick carefully, air valve facing the run up, and pointing slightly downwards
- Run straight at the ball, or from a narrow angle, whichever feels most comfortable
- Place the non-kicking foot beside the ball
- Arms for balance
- Strike ball with laces, and a clean, straight follow through
- Keep the body straight, head over the ball to keep the shot down

Technique: The Curler

The curler is perfect for clearing a wall and bending the ball into the corner of the goal. It is a case of sport meeting science. The Magnus Effect is the principle used. For those who wish to know, this is defined as the force exerted on a rapidly spinning sphere when it travels through the air. It provides force on the angle of direction related to that spin, and thereby causes the ball to curve.

However, exerting that spin with a human foot is easier said than done. The technique can be broken down into three areas. The run up, the contact and the follow through.

- The run up
    - This does not need to be too long. The shot is about control, not power
    - Each person can work out their own run up. A starting point is to take three steps directly back from the ball, then three steps to the side
    - Left footers should step to the right of the ball, right footers to the left

- The short run up to the shot will now be at an angle of around forty-five degrees
- Run up and place the non-kicking foot about twenty centimetres to the side of the ball
- Point the foot at about a forty-five-degree angle to the goal

- Contact
  - Strike the ball with the inside of the toes
  - Make contact close to the centre of the ball, but not exactly to the centre. Hit just below the middle, to give lift, and fractionally to the outside to impart spin
  - Lock the ankle on impact
  - Point the toes slightly upwards on impact
  - Practise until the right contact point for you is reached

- Follow through
  - Lean slightly over the ball
  - Follow through across the body to impart extra spin
  - Sometimes, players can gain extra control by not fully extending the follow through

The curler is not about power, it is about accuracy and deceit. Nevertheless, in order to beat a keeper, the more power that can be put in the better. However, technique comes first. Get that right, then the run up and force of strike can gradually be increased over time.

Drill/Tactic

As explained above, any free kick to be curled from in line with the penalty area will most likely be a direct shot on goal. (Remember, these are nearly twice as likely to result in a goal compared to a free kick taken as a cross). However, when the ball is wide a direct shot is not a serious option.

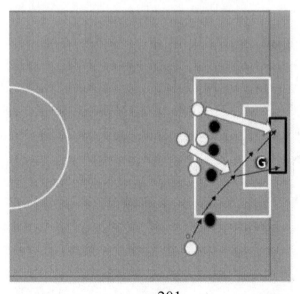

The free kick demonstrated above is a handy tool to acquire. It is a move on which coaches can work with positive results. The drill will help players perfect it. The ball is angled towards the middle of the goal, to bounce at this point. Strikers attack the near post. If they make contact with the ball, there is a good chance of a shot on target. However, if they do not reach the ball, it will often continue on its trajectory into the far corner of the net.

Normally, without the threat of a striker's run, a keeper will just dive and save the ball, but because they cannot commit to their dive until late, due to the possibility of that striker making near post or mid goal contact, the spin and bounce may take the ball past them and into the net.

Technique: The Chip

The chip shot is the curler's close family cousin. Genetically, they are almost the same, with a small number of significant differences. We've highlighted the differences in technique in italics in the description below.

- The run up

- o This does not need to be too long. The shot is about control, not power
- o Each person can work out their own run up. A starting point is to take three steps directly back from the ball, then *one or two* to the side
- o Left footers should step to the right of the ball, right footers to the left
- o *The short run up will be broadly straight*
- o Run up and place the non-kicking foot about twenty centimetres to the side of the ball
- o Point the foot *towards* the goal or target
- Contact
  - o Strike the ball with the inside of the toes
  - o Make contact in the centre of the ball, *but at its bottom* in order to give lift
  - o Lock the ankle on impact
  - o Point the toes slightly *downwards* on impact. This will impart lift and, crucially, the back spin which will cause the ball to dip
  - o Practise until the right contact point for you is reached
- Follow through
  - o Lean slightly *backwards to the ball*

- Follow through *straight and with control*
- Sometimes, players can gain extra control by not fully extending the follow through

The chip for goal will usually occur in open play, as keepers tend to stay on their line for free kicks. The tactic/drill below demonstrates how a chip can be a surprise tool for a defence expecting a free kick direct shot curler. Since the run ups for both are similar, the move can be disguised until the last minute.

Drill/Tactic – Chip Free Kick

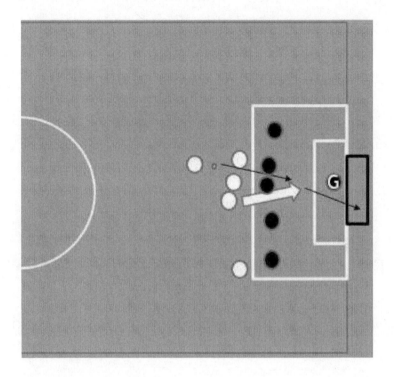

Here, the attacking place a wall in front of the defending wall. This is a common tactic when taking free kicks, especially now that recent rule changes forbid attackers to join in the defensive wall.

As the taker makes their run up, the outer player of the attacker's wall spins off, and heads into the gap between the outer player of the wall and the nearest marking defender. The defender in the wall cannot peel off to follow the run, since that will leave the wall vulnerable to a curler. The marking defender does not have time to get goal side of the runner.

The free kick taker chips the ball up and down over the wall (a tough skill, admittedly) and the striker runs onto the ball to hit a first time shot.

Tactic: Wide Attacking Free Kicks

This kind of free kick is really an advantageous corner and should be treated as such. As commentators often opine, as a full back makes a rash tackle, 'He's given away a dangerous free kick there…'

The one down side of a wide free kick over a corner is offside. However, late runs can render this ineffective for the defence.

Drill/Tactic: Defeating Offside

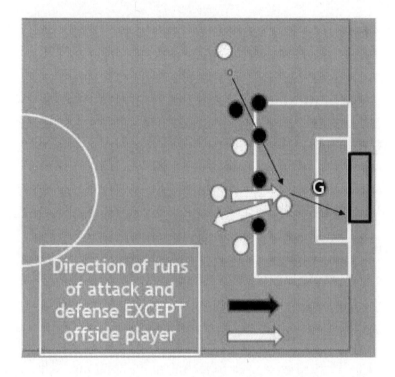

The drill sets up with the defence holding a high line, as would be the case in most matches. One attacker stands in an offside position towards the centre of the goal. As the kick is taken, this player retreats so they are not interfering with play. Meanwhile, a striker attacks from deep, aiming to be lost in the melee of attackers and defenders jostling for the ball.

If they get through, they have a relatively free shot on goal from close range.

This drill can only be used with age groups who play offside. Drill it from different angles.

<u>Here are the key points from the chapter</u>:

- Free kick specialists need a range of weapons in their armory
- Teams should develop players to provide this range of options
- From the coach's perspective, free kicks are either tactical exercises or technical undertakings where they involve a player taking a direct shot at goal

Our final chapter will take a look at an aspect of the game which is growing in significance. The role of statistics.

Some Statistics to Inform Tactics

'Sometimes in football, you have to score goals.' Thierry Henry

We can't claim that the findings below will guarantee winning strategies for coaches, but they are conclusions drawn from analysis of professional matches and competitions and offer a few pointers to where coaches can focus their tactics in order to create the best goalscoring opportunities.

Clearly, whether or not a team has the sorts of players to put these chances away is another factor entirely. Hopefully the coaching strategies outlined in the remainder of the book will assist players in becoming better finishers in order to put these additional chances away.

There are other caveats to consider. At an amateur or youth level, coaches are working with players who are, by definition, not as good as their professional counterparts. Defences are less organised and stable, dead ball skills are less developed, use of weaker foot and heading is less advanced. However, the findings are relevant because, for example, whilst our team might not be able to deliver a corner with quite the precision as Kevin De Bruyne, so our opponents are unlikely to have a Gerard Pique able to clear the ball away.

Statistic: From Where are goals scored?

Data suggests that the split between goals scored from open play and those scored from set pieces is around 70/30. Some studies suggest that it could be as close as 60/40. At an amateur level, the figure is likely to sit further apart due to the quality of set piece delivery, but at the same time, defences may be less able to cope with a set piece threat.

Implication: There is strong evidence to suggest that specific set play tactics and training should form a part of a coach's overall plan.

Statistic: Set Piece Break Down

Perhaps it is not surprising that the highest percentage of goals from set plays come from penalties. Undoubtedly, the figure would be higher were penalties to be a more frequent aspect of the game.

Implication: From an offensive viewpoint, it is worthwhile training three or four players to be specialist penalty takers. Youth coaches might expand on this number, because kids like nothing more than taking penalties. It is probably not worth spending time working with more players in adult settings, simply because the overwhelming likelihood is that other players will not ever take a penalty. The exception being those rare leagues where drawn matches are settled by penalty shoot-out. Even then, stats suggest that draws are pretty unlikely in amateur settings.

Taking a purely random league in the hope of illustrating the point, we found that in the first thirty three games of the Wharfside Electrical Milton Keynes Sunday Football League (yes, that one) only two were draws. Although the percentage might be higher in a cup competition, where a shoot-out may become the deciding factor, it will still be unlikely that one results.

After penalties the next most likely goal scoring set pieces are corners and free kicks, accounting for just under a third of goals each. (Penalties being responsible for just over a third, so all three set pieces are important.) Finally, throw ins rarely lead directly to goals. Even the mighty Tony Pulis/Rory Delap long throw routine at Stoke City yielded just eighteen goals in nearly seven seasons. (Pulis explained it was more about getting the crowd wound up and intimidating opponents, not something easy to do on an Adelaide Park on a Sunday morning).

Implications: Offensively, in terms of goal scoring, equal time should be spent on free kicks and corners, working on routines and involving full squad participation. There is little need to work on throw ins unless a specific problem or opportunity (e.g., having a player with a particularly long throw and flat trajectory) arises.

The point about corners is one which leads to much debate. On the one hand, only about one in thirty corners leads to a goal, which might not seem enough to commit time to the aspect of the game, On the other, a team might win five or six corners per match – more if they are on top. That equates to a goal every five or six games. Enough to justify time spent in training.

Statistic: Open Play Break Down

Conclusions in this section are inevitably influenced by trends in the game. The high press is very popular at the time of writing. On the one hand, history suggests that trends are transitory, coaches adopting new ideas once defences work out how to negate the current fashion. On the other, a trend would not gain purchase if it did not work.

To that end, the high press works at the moment. In the professional game, we are seeing a softer approach to this as opposing defences and goalkeepers become more adept with their footballing skills and can play around the press to exploit the spaces in behind it. Often now the press is triggered by certain circumstances. That may be a player on the ball who is identified as being technically weaker than their teammates, or the ball originating from a certain position. For example, a ball that has been played in behind the full back and centre half causing them to turn.

However, it is not surprising that latest figures suggest the highest percentage of goals come when an attack begins in the attacking third. That in turn implies a situation where the ball is won far up the pitch. However, the difference is neither overwhelming nor decisive, with statistically insignificant fewer goals coming from attacks which begin in the defending or middle thirds.

Implication: This would seem to suggest that most chances are created from a high press. However, not sufficiently high a percentage to adopt tactics around this approach irrespective of the strengths and weaknesses of our team. A high press is a risky endeavour if done badly. A good coach will build their strategy around the strengths of the players they have, whilst simultaneously trying to improve skills to allow them to operate with a stronger tactic once their players have the technical skills to play in this way.

Far more significant than where an attack begins is what happens to lead to a goal. Here, the evidence is strongly in favour of a short passing strategy. Statistics suggest that well over two thirds of goals from open play are generated in this way. In contrast, little more than one in ten goals come from a long ball pass. (Enough to suggest teams hold this variety in their arsenal, just that they should not use it often.)

The modern game is built around the short pass, with perhaps Barcelona and Spain's tika taka soccer of the mid to late noughties and early 2010s being the perfect illustration. Not only was this soccer wonderful to watch, but it was extremely successful. In contrast, England's strategy of the decades following their disappointments of not qualifying for the 1974 and 1978 World Cups was built largely on the strategies of Charles Hughes, their Director of Coaching. His book, The Winning Formula, became the Bible upon which many successive England managers relied, and failed. Perhaps overlooking that not every soccer playing nation performed on the farm fields that graced the English game, he eschewed technical skills for statistical analysis and tactical simplicity. Through studying numerous matches (well, over a hundred) he concluded two things. Firstly, most goals came from delivering the final pass from certain areas of the pitch, which he called POMO, or positions of maximum opportunity. These were largely wide areas and required accurate crosses into the box and a big centre forward who could finish the chance. Secondly, he believed that to have the best chance of scoring there needed to be no more than three passes before the attempt on goal ensued.

It is not hard to see why this failed. By definition, to get the ball from front to back in three passes requires long passes. These are harder to play and easier to defend against than short, accurate passes. So attacks broke down too easily. His ideas owed much to the findings of Charles Reep, who was a Wing Commander during the second world, a fan of Swindon Town and a former accountant (all vital characteristics of a football analyst).

Of course, England during the seventies and eighties, plus much of the nineties, were pretty atrocious. Their soccer was lumpen compared to the silky skills and progressive tactics of the likes of Brazil, Argentina, Germany (including West Germany), Italy and, later, France. However, we make the point to illustrate that even flawed tactics might hold some benefits. Rapid passing and getting the ball forward quicky does lead to goals, provided the ball is won far enough up the pitch. It is the knockout punch attached to the end of a high press.

Implications: The best coaches develop technique in their players by working on key personal skills. First touch, control, receiving the ball on the half turn, playing controlled, short passes. By developing technique in this way, especially with the youngest players, coaches turn their soccer players into better finishers. This is because the skills of finishing under pressure also require the sort of excellent technique drilled into players from this early age.

Statistic: The Most Likely Time to Score

A lot more goals are scored in the second half compared to the first. In the 2018 World Cup, for example, almost two thirds of goals came after half time. Interestingly, we might assume that as the game goes on, and players become more tired, so the incidences of goals increase. That is not absolutely true. Although a lot are scored in the final fifteen minutes, most, it seems, occur in the fifteen minutes after half time.

Maybe coaches do make a difference, and their half time instructions do lead to goals.

Implications: It is difficult to draw too many conclusions because a number of factors come into play. As the game progresses so more players might be on a yellow card, and must therefore be more wary of their tackling, for example. Substitutes are more likely to have come on, further altering the ebb and flow of the game. The best implication to draw is that having fresh legs in attack may well lead to more goals in the latter stages of the game. On the other hand, of course, if the player was that good, they may well have started. Perhaps the answer lies in tactically loading the offense towards the latter stages of a game. This conclusion being reached on the twin factors of a defence in any case being more likely to make mistakes towards the end of the match, and the related conclusion that it makes sense to have extra attackers around to exploit this.

We are not sure we would trust this conclusion sufficiently to base a coaching strategy on it! Nevertheless, we do often see the 'fresh legs' approach being used in the professional game, with strikers swapped in the final thirty minutes.

<u>Here are the key points from the chapter</u>:

- Statistically, there are tactics which will lead to the creation of more chances
- Nevertheless, we must consider the strengths (and deficiencies) of our players when deciding on our tactics
- Set plays are important and can lead to the scoring of a significant number of goals. Therefore, drills on set plays will deliver rewards
- Technique is all
- Good coaches and players will understand the game better through a study of statistics and their conclusions

Conclusion

'Everyone talks about the forwards, the players when they are scoring goals. But sometimes I look for the complete player not just the players who score but those who can pass.' Pele.

The great man's words are true. There are many who argue that the traditional finisher's days are numbered, even past. The 'false nine', developed by the great Spain sides of the late noughties, began the trend. Now even players such as Harry Kane or Robert Lewandowski, great finishers both, offer much more from their game than just putting the ball in the net.

Look at teams across the world, the best teams, and rarely do they play a traditional, old school center forward. Take Liverpool or Manchester City, the strongest teams in the English Premier League, widely accepted now as the most competitive league in world football. Neither has an out and out center forward. For Liverpool, Sadio Mane and, especially, Mo Salah, score most of their goals. But these are wide players, who have a major duty tracking back.

Roberto Firmino or Diego Jota are the central men. Both, especially Jota, score regularly enough. Neither are particularly prolific though.

Manchester City frequently play without a number nine altogether. Goals come from all over the pitch.

This means that every player in the team, with the probable exception of the goalkeeper, is now expected to be an effective finisher. The days of attackers and defenders training separately, or the defense's role being to offer some opposition to the strikers in practice, are over. That's a good thing. Surely.

Because it means that at the younger levels, all players are learning about all aspects of the game. Players are not being lost because specialization takes place too early. Everybody needs to understand defense; every player must be able to fulfil the role of a midfielder, and every single outfield participant in the game must develop their skills as a finisher.

The end… almost!

Reviews are not easy to come by.

As an independent author with a tiny marketing budget, I rely on readers, like you, to leave a short review on Amazon.

Even if it's just a sentence or two!

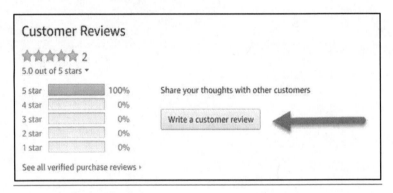

I am very appreciative for your review as it truly makes a difference.

Thank you from the bottom of my heart for purchasing this book and reading it to the end.

Made in the USA
Middletown, DE
21 December 2024

67982290R00124